The Family Camping Guide: How to Survive a Camping Trip (and Have Fun Doing It)

by Rashelle Davis

<u>Disclaimer:</u>

While we endeavor to keep the information in this book up to date and correct, we make no representations or warranties of any kind, express or implied, about the completeness, accuracy, reliability, suitability or availability with respect to the book or the information, products, services, or related graphics contained book for any purpose. Any reliance you place on such information is therefore strictly at your own risk.

In no event will we be liable for any liability, loss or damage including without limitation, indirect or consequential loss or damage, or any loss or damage whatsoever arising from loss of data or profits arising out of, or in connection with, the use of the material or the interpretation of the material contained in this book.

Dedication:

This book is dedicated to all the campers out there, especially those who have endured the bee stings, poison oak and ivy and the constant barrage of pests and had a great time regardless.

Contents

Introduction 10

Start Small and Build On It 14

First Time Camper Programs 17

An Experienced Friend Can Make All the Difference
.... 20

Backyard Camping: How to Camp Out with All the
Comforts of Home 22

The Devil's In the Details: How to Plan a Camping Trip
.... 26

Picking a Destination 27

What Do You Want to Look At? 27

Quiet Folks vs. Party Animals 29

Types of Campgrounds 31

Take Your Search Online 33

Reserve Your Site 37

Water Can Be Very Good or Very Bad 40

The Long Walk 42

The "Boat" Launch 44

Playing in Traffic 48

A Little Space, Please 49

Shady Acres 50

Do You Need Utilities? 51

First Come, First Serve... 53

Choosing a Campsite When There Are No Boundaries
.... 55

Triple Check Your List... 59

Essential Camping Gear: There's No Need to Break the
Bank 64

Shelter.. 66

Tent Types... 69

Sleeping Bags 72

Bag Shapes 74

Fill Materials: It's What's On the Inside that Counts
.... 75

Storing Your Sleeping Bag 76

Sleeping Pads 78

Let There Be Light 80

Fuel Lanterns.................................... 80

Electric Lanterns 81

Flashlights 82

Keeping It Cool: The Ice Chest............................. 84

Tips for Keeping Things Cold............................ 85

First Aid: What You Need in Your Kit 87

Dress for Success 90

The Art of Layering................................ 94

Family Camping Safety 96

Beat the Heat 97

Avoid Campsite Hazards 100

Set Clear Boundaries 103

Beware the Silent Killer 104

It's OK to Have Some Fun 106

Go Hiking 108

Before the Trip 116

During the Trip 117

What to Do If You're Lost 118

Hit the Water 121

Boating 121

Diving and Snorkeling 121

Fishing 122

Float around 122

Rafting 122

Skipping rocks 123

Swimming 123

Sports and Recreational Games 124

Baseball 124

Bike riding 124

Capture the flag 124

Corn hole 125

Disc golf 126

Football 126

Hide and Seek 126

Horseshoes 127

Ladder toss 128

Lawn bowling 128

Rock climbing 128

Soccer.. 128

Spelunking 129

Tag... 129

Washers 131

Card Games 133

Go Fish.. 133

Liar 134

Old Maid 135

Slap Jack.. 136

Spoons 136

UNO 138

War.. 138

Cooking While Camping 140

Camp Stoves... 141

Charcoal Barbecues 144

The Charcoal Chimney 145

Charcoal Grilling Tips.. 146

Direct and Indirect Grilling.................................. 146

Wood Fire....................................... 148

Campfire Cooking Tips........................... 149

The Campfire: An Age-Old Tradition....................... 151

Campfire Fun....................................... 154

Camping Recipes 156

Bacon, Egg, Sausage and Potato Omelet 157

Balsamic Barbecued Steak 158

BBQ Beef Ribs 159

BBQ Chicken 161

Beans and Franks................................ 163

Breakfast Burritos.............................. 164

Campfire Baked Potato 165

Clam Chowder................................... 166

Dutch oven Baked Beans 168

Dutch Oven Cinnamon Caramel Monkey Bread.... 170

Dutch Oven Chili Macaroni 171

Dutch Oven Fruit Pie............................ 172

Eggs in a Nest.................................. 174

Fire-Roasted Cinnamon Apple.................... 175

Five Alarm Dutch Oven Chili 176

Killer Kabobs 178

Quick and Easy Pancakes........................ 180

Traditional Banana Boat......................... 182

Let's Hear Your Camping Stories 183

Introduction

"We should go camping."

Four simple words that strike fear into the hearts of city-dwelling mothers everywhere.

Don't get me wrong . . . Camping can be fun and is a great way to introduce young children to the outdoors. It's just that young children are hard enough to watch at home, where everything is childproofed and safe (for the most part). Taking a family to spend the night in the woods (or the desert, beach, lake, river or anywhere else someone decided to place a campsite) opens an entire world of new hazards that must be avoided.

The insects are bigger and badder than those us city folk are used to. Fire ants, yellow jackets, wasps and mosquitoes big enough to carry your youngest child away to their nest to feed to their young are all hazards that must be avoided. OK, maybe I exaggerated a bit on the last one, but I swear I saw a mosquito the size of a small hummingbird the last time I let my husband talk me into going camping.

Then there are the wild animals. You've got animals that specialize in lurking in the shadows and waiting until everyone's fast asleep before sneaking into the middle of the campsite to raid the food supply. You've also got aquatic animals, reptiles and all sorts of creatures wandering about that need to be avoided. Sure, we've all heard the saying they're more scared of us than we are of them in regard to wild animals, but I don't think that applies to a bear that happens upon a campsite full of tasty morsels.

As if the wild animals and insects on steroids aren't enough, there are a number of other hazards that present a threat. Just to name a few, you've got deep water packed with vegetation, steep cliffs and ravines, rogue waves capable of washing a small child out to sea and quicksand. OK, maybe quicksand is a bit of a stretch, but I've seen the other three—and they were all at a single campsite!

It's enough to drive a slightly neurotic parent insane. As if there isn't enough to worry about at home, we now have to follow our family out into the wilderness where we're still expected to keep a watchful eye on our wayward children and make sure they make it home in one piece. Camping is easy for the men. All they have to do is set up a few tents, light a fire here and there and maybe barbecue some food. While they're out "working hard" catching dinner it's our job to make sure there are children left alive to eat it when they return.

Then there are the unsanitary restrooms and showers, if the campsite you're at has such extravagancies. Running water isn't guaranteed while camping. Neither is electricity. If your idea of roughing it is spending the night at a Best Western instead of the Marriot, you're in for a rude awakening when you go camping for the first time.

If you're feeling particularly adventurous, you can forgo the niceties of a normal campground and blaze your own trail, camping out in an undeveloped area. I've tried it, and while there's something to be said about being at one with nature, I find myself constantly wondering *what happens if the car doesn't start*? If that were to occur, I would end up hundreds of miles from the nearest living, breathing soul, with only my husband's survival skills, most of which he gleaned from a single Survivor Man Marathon, to keep us alive. While he might be comfortable with that, I can undoubtedly say I'm not, which is the reason I now require we camp somewhere other people will find our bodies in the morning if we don't make it through the night.

While anyone who has experience camping knows pretty much everything I've written so far is a stretch of the imagination, that's how I felt when I first started camping with my family—and I'm sure there are others out there who feel exactly the same right at this very moment. I felt there was danger lurking around every corner and that I had to be on the constant lookout for said danger. While there are some things you need to look out for, camping doesn't have to be a miserable experience the mere mention of which sends a chill up your spine.

The fact of the matter is hundreds of thousands of campers enjoy spending time outdoors each and every year and grave injuries and deaths are extremely rare. I think it's more the fear of the unknown that terrifies mothers new to the world of camping. That, and the inability to wake up to a warm shower in the comfort of their own home. That part I'll never get used to.

This may come as a surprise, but camping can actually be fun. Do it enough times and do it the right way and you might actually get good at it and start to enjoy and look forward to camping trips. There's something to be said about leaving civilization behind and heading out somewhere to get in touch with nature. Sleeping with nothing between you and the great outdoors but a thin piece of canvas can at time be a bit scary, like when raccoons raid your campsite and raise a racket, but it can also be downright peaceful and relaxing.

"We should go camping."

Learn to camp the right way and you might find you're the one saying those four words. Instead of dreading the day your husband utters them, you'll be pestering him to schedule another trip to the lake or to the beach before all the campsites fill up. Camping can be a great time. It's a great bonding experience for the family and is a great way to escape the daily grind.

The Family Camping Guide is crafted from the cumulative experience of myself and a number of others who all dreaded camping at one point in time, but have now learned to love it . . . or at least like it . . . or at least tolerate it. Well, you get the point. If you want to enjoy your family camping trips, this is the book for you. It covers everything from picking a site to quick and easy recipes the whole family will love.

Start Small and Build On It

No matter how much you read up on camping, you aren't going to become an expert until you've actually gone out and got a camping trip or two under your belt. One of the biggest mistakes rookie campers make is biting off more than they can chew the first few trips they take.

Instead of taking an easy trip somewhere close to home, they read up on camping and decide to take a week-long trip into the middle of nowhere. They get out to their campsite and realize they're in way over their head and decide camping isn't for them. More often than not, the trip ends up having to be cut short because something happened that the new campers weren't prepared to handle. You see it all the time. There's next to new camping gear being sold in classified ads constantly, usually the result of one of these misguided trips gone so wrong the family decides camping isn't for them.

The best advice I can give you is to start off with small, manageable trips to developed campsites close to home.

A weekend trip is a good start for most new campers. I'd recommend going for three days the first time you camp. This gives you a day to get there and get set up, a day to relax and have fun and a day to pack up and head home. An overnight trip may seem like a better idea to some, but it can seem like a grind because you don't have much time to yourself. There isn't any time to relax because you're setting up camp the first day, which can take quite some time, especially if you're setting things up for the first time. The next day is spent taking everything down and packing up, leaving you feeling like the only thing you did was set your tents up and then take them down.

If you're on a weekend trip to a site close to home and something goes wrong and the trip ends up a disaster, you'll be able to write it off as a lesson learned without having wasted a ton of money and time planning it. A shorter trip that doesn't work out isn't as huge of a disappointment as a larger, more expensive trip. Most families can only afford one or two large trips a year, so save those trips for later on down the road when you have the experience and peace of mind to enjoy them.

There's another benefit to taking a shorter trip the first time out. Camping isn't for everyone and if you get out there and hate every minute of it, you won't be stuck for days on end. A couple days of camping is tolerable for even the most princess-like of divas. Extend that out to a week and it can seem like a grind.

Start off small with a 3-day trip.

If you enjoy it, you can do the same type of trip again the next time or, if things went well and you think you're ready, you can try staying for 4 or 5 days the next time around. I used to push for shorter camping trips because I hated every miserable minute of them. Now, I'm the one pushing for an extra few days to relax.

Once you get the hang of things, 5 to 7 day trips will be a breeze. Starting off with a trip that long is a recipe for disaster, unless you've got experienced campers staying with you the whole time who are willing to help you out along the way. Unless you're really sure you're going to enjoy camping, I'd still go small at first. It's like learning to drive a car in a way. You aren't going to learn to drive by hopping behind the wheel of a Lamborghini. You're going to start in a smaller car and (hopefully) one day work up to driving a Lambo. Start with smaller camping trips and work your way up to the bigger ones as you learn the ropes.

First Time Camper Programs

For those who have never gone camping and don't know a tent pole from a fishing pole, first time camping programs can be a great way to get your feet wet without jumping headfirst into the deep end. A number of state and regional park programs have programs designed to get people new to the world of camping started down the path to outdoor success.

These programs usually entail a group of new campers embarking on guided camping trips where there are experts on-hand to help out when the unexpected happens. The experts teach the group the fundamentals of camping in a group setting where everyone in the group is inexperienced and likely to experience similar problems. Some programs offer more in-depth training in areas like fishing, hiking, canoeing and other recreational activities unique to the area where the guided camping trip takes place. These programs are great because you're camping with a group that's every bit as inexperienced as you are and you don't have to worry about asking stupid questions.

Some programs even have gear you can borrow or purchase on the cheap. The better programs team up with local outfitters to provide great prices on entry-level tents, sleeping bags and other gear you'll need to survive. Other programs have loaner gear that can be checked out and borrowed for the trip. The gear has to be returned after the trip, but it's a good choice for families not sure whether camping is their thing. Fully outfitting your family with even the least expensive camping gear can cost hundreds, if not thousands of dollars. Loaner programs allow you to experience camping without the initial financial output. If you like it, you can buy your own gear later on down the road.

The North Face company has teamed up with a number of park and recreation groups across the country to offer first time camping programs. They currently offer programs in the following areas:

- **Bay Area State Parks, California.**
- **Chicago Park District, Illinois.**
- **Colorado State Parks.**
- **Georgia State Parks.**
- **Idaho State Parks.**
- **Maryland State Parks.**
- **Massachusetts State Parks.**
- **Michigan State Parks.**
- **Missouri State Parks.**
- **New York State Parks.**
- **Ohio State Parks.**
- **Oregon State Parks.**
- **Pennsylvania State Parks.**

This program offers different services at each location. If you live near one of the above locations and are interested, check what's available near you at the following web address:

http://www.exploreyourparks.com/camping101/

Let me state that I am not affiliated with the North Face company in any way, shape or form. I just think this is a great program to help people get started camping and it is a great choice for first-timers if it's available in your area. If not, contact your local and state park organizations to see if similar programs are available in your area.

An Experienced Friend Can Make All the Difference

We all have a friend from high school who's gotten into survival prepping. You know the guy I'm talking about . . . Yes, the one who spends months on end in the woods learning survival skills so he'll be prepared when the world as we know it comes to a crashing halt. For most of us, this friend is the extent of our survival plan in an extended emergency. If a meteor hits the planet and blacks out ¾ of the United States, we plan on heading to this friend's house with kids in tow.

The good news is this prepper friend is a great person to take along camping.

As long as your friend is safe to have around your kids, this guy is a great choice to invite along on your first camping trip or two, as long as you can tolerate his rants about anything and everything conspiracy. He's spent years learning to survive on the contents of a single bag. A camping trip is like a luxury night out on the town. He'll know exactly what to do when your propane cook stove won't light on the first night or the kids crash into the tent and break two of the poles.

He'll also be more than willing to fight off any wild animals that wander their way into your campsite. Just be prepared to politely turn down the raccoon stew or bobcat kabobs he makes out of his fresh kill.

If you don't have a survivalist prepper friend, a friend with a few camping trips under his or her belt is the next best thing. While a friend like this isn't likely to engage in hand to paw combat with an angry wolverine to save your life, he can show you how to set up and take down tents and will be able to guide you gently along the path to camping self-sufficiency.

Nothing is easy the first time you camp out. Having a friend along who knows how to properly build a campfire and light a lantern can make life much easier—and the trip will be less stressful on everyone involved because you won't end up arguing with your significant other because they didn't read the instructions on the tent before it got too dark outside to see.

If you don't have an experienced friend you can bring along, at the very least go with a group of people. If there's something you aren't able to figure out, maybe the collective brainpower of the group can figure it out. Maybe not, but there's a better chance of someone stumbling across a solution when there are more people trying to come up with one. If not, you can all laugh about it over a few cocktails once the kids have bedded down in the back seat of the car because you couldn't figure out how to set up the new tent you took out of the box for the first time 10 minutes before the sun went down.

Backyard Camping: How to Camp Out with All the Comforts of Home

I have a friend who absolutely detests camping. She can't go a whole day without the comforts of home. She loves her hair dryer, her walk-in closet and her big-screen TV too much to leave it behind and set off on a camping trip to a place that doesn't have such amenities. The thought of camping out somewhere she might encounter such terrifying creatures as a raccoon or a scorpion makes her literally sick to her stomach.

Her kids love camping and beg her to take them on camping trips during the summer. They enjoy sleeping in tents and being outdoors. They're the exact polar opposite of their mother and they tend to be very vocal about wanting to head outdoors. My husband and I have volunteered to take the kids with us on one of our yearly trips, but my friend isn't too keen on sending her kids out into the great unknown. I suspect she thinks we allow our children to run around completely unsupervised while half-naked and painted with war paint on our family trips. To be fair, she's never voiced this concern, but it's written all over her face when she politely turns down our invitation.

A few years back, after countless arguments with her husband and children about the fun they were missing out on because she wouldn't go camping, my friend stumbled across a solution to her problems: backyard camping. By camping out in her backyard, she could take the kids camping while staying close to the comforts of home. If she got tired of hanging out in the backyard, she could temporarily suspend the camping trip and head inside, where she could take a hot shower, make a cup of coffee and relax on the couch while catching up on her favorite shows.

By staying within walking distance of her back door, she was able to tolerate camping out while keeping the kids happy. All she had to buy was a tent, a couple cheap sleeping bags and an air mattress. She also bought a couple flashlights, so the kids could have fun exploring the backyard at night. Now that the kids are older, she lets them camp in the yard while she gets a good night's sleep in her bed, which is 20 feet from where the tents are set up. She sleeps with the window open and can hear everything the kids are up to on their "camping" trip.

Be sure to notify the neighbors of your plans, because flashlights flickering around backyards in urban areas in the middle of the night aren't usually associated with backyard camping trips. Imagine my friend's surprise when 3 squad cars pulled up in front of her house expecting multiple burglars prowling around her yard. It ended well, with her and the kind officers having a good laugh about the 8-, 10- and 12-year old "burglars" they'd been sent out to apprehend. The officers laughed it off, but were sure to point out that things could have ended differently had they have been on edge and one of the kids jumped out at them from the dark.

When it comes to backyard camping, you make the rules.

Some people treat it like a real camping trip, where everything they need is kept in their "campsite" and they aren't allowed to go in the house during their camping trip, except for emergencies and to use the bathroom. Others keep the food in the fridge and go inside during the heat of the day to relax and shower.

During the day, you can head to a nearby park or nature area and go exploring and hiking like you would on a normal camping trip. Don't forget the cameras and binoculars, so your kids will be able to experience nature close up and document their trip.

A backyard camping trip can be a fun way to keep the kids busy while they're out of school. Pitch the tents or, if weather allows, let the kids sleep out under the stars. Most kids love backyard camping trips because they're a break from the norm. We go on a handful of real camping trips every year and my kids still love to camp out in the backyard from time to time during the summer.

Backyard camping can also be a great way to take a dry run camping trip close to home. You can set everything up and spend the night in your yard to learn the ropes and make sure you know how to use all of your gear and it works correctly. If something doesn't work right or you have a problem, the comfort of your own home is but a few short steps away.

The best part about backyard camping is it allows you time to bond with your family. While most families spend a good portion of the day doing their own thing while at home, a backyard camping trip creates a venue in which the entire family works together in order to ensure the campsite is prepped and all the daily chores and activities are completed. Be sure to include fun stuff like roasting marshmallows around a campfire or nature hikes through the neighborhood or the camping experience won't be a fun one for the children. You can also eliminate normal bedtimes and let the children stay up as late as they want, as long as they agree to stay in the tent. Let them invite a friend or two over for the camping trip and they'll have even more fun.

Make sure young children know you're just a step or two away if they get scared and want some comfort at night. Backyard camping is generally safe, but nighttime noises can be scary for younger children regardless of where they're camping out at.

Do it right and a backyard camping trip can be every bit as memorable as a real camping trip—and you'll never have to leave the comforts of home behind.

The Devil's In the Details: How to Plan a Camping Trip

A successful camping trip starts long before you actually get to the campsite and set up. It starts in the comfort of your own home, where you need to do a good bit of planning in order to make sure your trip isn't ruined before it gets underway. The best-planned trips are usually the most successful trips.

By planning, I don't mean laying out a minute-by-minute itinerary of what you're going to do on the trip. A fun and successful camping trip isn't planned out down to the last roasted marshmallow. There's a certain amount of going with the flow that's required, no matter how OCD you tend to be at home.

What I do mean is planning ahead when it comes to what you're going to bring and what you're going to do. When the kids say they're cold, hungry or bored, you'll already have a plan in place. Let's take a look at the planning you're going to need to do well in advance of your trip in order to ensure everything is in order when the big day arrives.

Picking a Destination

It sounds simple enough, choosing a place to camp.

It should be easy, right? If you've seen one campground, you've seen them all. Pick a spot, set up camp and you'll be good to go.

If only it were that easy.

Let me get one common misconception out of the way right off the bat. Not all campgrounds are created equal, and campsites within a campground can vary in quality considerably. The people that stay at campgrounds aren't created equal, either. Determining what kind of person you are and what sort of campground you want to stay at before you start looking will allow you to find a good match for your family.

Here are some of the choices you're going to have to make when selecting a campground.

What Do You Want to Look At?

This first consideration is probably the most important one of all. What do you want to look at while you're camping? What makes you happy? What scenery will put you in the best mood? If you hate sun and sand, going camping at the beach in the middle of summer probably isn't a good idea. If you hate snow, a cabin in the winter will be miserable. On the other hand, you might be a beach or snow bunny and love these locations.

It's all about finding the best place for you.

For some, the beach, with its rolling waves and sand dunes will be the place of choice. For others, there's nothing better than fresh air and the sound of a babbling brook nearby. If you're as lucky as I am, you have literally almost every terrain imaginable within a day's drive. I could drive an hour and stay on the beach one trip and then drive a few hours in the other direction and stay by a lake in the High Sierras the next. The high desert lies to the south and I've got a bunch of lakes, reservoirs and rivers sandwiched in between. I could literally be fishing in a river in 65 to 70 degree weather in the morning and decide I want to go skiing and be on the slopes by the afternoon.

Here are some of the destinations you might consider planning a trip to:

- **Beaches.**
- **Deltas.**
- **Deserts.**
- **Islands.**
- **Jungle.**
- **Lakes.**
- **Mountains.**
- **Rivers.**
- **Streams.**
- **Wilderness areas.**
- **Woods.**

Wherever you find outdoor recreation opportunities, be it by a hilly area, a beach or near a body of water, chances are there's a campground nearby. Pick a destination you're interested in and where you'll enjoy the view. Don't shoehorn yourself into a campsite where you hate the view. Find a place you'll enjoy camping with something you want to look at and you'll have a much better time.

My children used to beg my mother to go camping with us. She's 65 years old and in excellent shape, so camping isn't out of the question for her. She used to complain that there isn't anything she wants to see around a campsite. When my kids asked what she likes to look at while on vacation, she jokingly told them penny slot machines. Imagine her surprise when I found a casino with a campground right next to it. She went camping with us on a trip to the casino campground and spent most of her days sitting in the air conditioned casino—and had a blast doing it.

Quiet Folks vs. Party Animals

There are two basic types of campers: those who are peaceful and quiet and are ready to turn in around 9PM and those who raucously party until all hours of the night.

The peaceful, quiet folks are great people to camp around if you're looking for a serene stay at a quiet campground. You'll be able to turn in early, knowing your neighbors are going to do the same. A campground that caters to quiet people tends to either be full of families that don't party hard once the kids have gone to bed or fishermen who plan on getting up at the crack of dawn to head out to a favorite honey hole.

This sort of campground is great if you're the type who's in bed by 9 or 10 PM and want a peaceful night's sleep. It isn't great if you're planning on staying up and partaking of adult beverages after hours. No matter how quiet you plan on being, it won't be quiet enough when you're surrounded by people trying to get a good night's sleep.

If you're curious as to how strict a campground is when it comes to noise, ask what their noise ordinances are and how strictly they're enforced.

Strict enforcement of noise ordinances can be a bit of a double-edged sword. I once stayed at a campground where a state park ranger stalked the campground at night with his flashlight off. He'd creep up on each site and then threaten to arrest anyone he heard making what he thought was too much noise. I'm pretty sure the guy got picked on by the "cool kids" at school when he was younger and this was his revenge. He didn't strictly enforce noise ordinances insomuch as he made the campground his personal prison camp and sought to make anyone who dared violate the sanctity of his camp miserable to the point they packed up and left.

If you enjoy a cocktail or two (or ten) while you stay up until the wee hours of the morning, you more than likely fall into the party animal camp. Party campgrounds are usually loud, obnoxious places, but they can be fun if that's what you're looking for. Just don't expect to the put the kids to bed early. They'll be kept awake by the hooting and hollering going around you. To be completely honest with you, staying at one of these campgrounds is best done without children in tow. Drunken campers can get a bit reckless and their behavior might endanger your children.

If you're the reckless type, then by all means stay at one of these sites. Don't go somewhere quiet and ruin it for everyone there.

The problem with party animals vs. quiet folks is it's usually an all-or-nothing type of thing. You probably aren't going to find a campsite full of people willing to go to bed at the exact time you want to go to bed. You also aren't going to find a campsite full of people who care whether your kids are bedding down for the night. Tents are made of thin material and even a quiet group that stays up late can sound like they're sitting around your tent talking and laughing.

Luckily, there's a third option when it comes to choosing between a loud or quiet campground and that's to head out to a remote camping location where you can set up so far from other campers it doesn't matter what you do. Places like this usually allow camping in large swaths of land, so you can pick a spot a good distance away from everyone else. You'll be able to be as loud or as quiet at night as you want and there won't be anyone around to care one way or the other.

Types of Campgrounds

Franchise campgrounds are typically large cookie cutter campgrounds that are expensive to stay at, but offer amenities many of the smaller campgrounds don't have. Franchise campgrounds are typically owned by individuals who purchase the rights to use the franchise name because of the advertising opportunities it opens up to them. KOA and Jellystone are both large franchises with campgrounds spread across the nation.

The extra money you spend usually nets you extra amenities. Many of the franchise campgrounds offer Internet service, swimming pools, on-site general stores, Laundromats and a number of other services you may or may not find at a private campground.

Private campgrounds usually cost less money, but don't always have the same amenities. They are often, but not always, smaller than the franchise campgrounds and tend to offer a more personable experience.

This isn't always the case, and most campgrounds are only as good as the person in charge.

I always call ahead with questions, just to see the attitude of those in charge. Ask to speak to the person who runs the camp. If you get the runaround, you'll know you're dealing with a company where the person in charge doesn't want to be bothered with the day to day responsibilities of running a campground. At the smaller campgrounds, the owner of the campground will often be the one who answers the phones. If the person is polite and more than happy to answer any questions you have, you may be in for a good experience. On the other hand, if the person you speak to is rude and stand-offish, you might be in for a rough trip, especially if problems related to the campsite take place.

Government-owned campgrounds are owned by a government agency and can be under the control of local, state or federal agencies. They sometimes license control of the campground to a private company that is placed in charge of the daily operation of the campground.

State and county campgrounds run the gamut from really nice campgrounds that give the franchise campgrounds a run for their money to tiny campgrounds with no amenities at all. I've found state campgrounds tend to be a bit nicer than county campgrounds, due to the fact the states usually have more funding and the campgrounds are designed to handle large numbers of people.

State forest campgrounds tend to be rough and rugged, but offer peace and solitude for those looking to get away from the grind. The sites are usually free (or charge a nominal usage fee), but there are no amenities. You bring everything you need and you're pretty much on your own. National park campsites are few and far between, but tend to be great places to camp—and they're usually located near National points of attraction, so you'll have plenty of stuff to do while you're camping.

If you have an RV, you have a few more options than those of us camping in tents. You can stay at many Wal-Mart's across the nation. There are also a number of travel plazas and even some casinos that offer free camping. Then again, if you have an RV, you're more than likely a seasoned camping vet and aren't reading this book.

Take Your Search Online

In the old days, people were extremely limited when it came time to find a campground. There were a handful of campsite directory books available that listed some, but nowhere near all of the campgrounds around the United States. Most campgrounds were chosen by word of mouth. If a friend stayed at a campground and recommended it, people would call Information, get the number to the campground and reserve a spot.

Now, there's a wealth of information at your fingertips. You can go online using either a computer or a smartphone and find out every last detail about pretty much any campsite across the United States.

Most campgrounds have websites you can check out, but don't stop your search there. Many of the websites feature outdated pictures that show the campground in its heyday. Many a camper has arrived at a campground that looked brand new in the pictures to find it hasn't been updated in the last 20 years. Picking a campsite based on pictures on the campground's website is a lot like picking a mate based solely on photographs on a dating website. You'll see the campground at the best it's ever looked, but may arrive to find the pictures you used to choose the site are outdated and don't represent the current condition of the site.

I once picked a campground based on pictures in a brochure I'd picked up at an outdoors show. I arrived at the campground to find the swimming pool I'd been so excited about had been filled in with dirt and paved over. The large sites full of green grass were now filled with dirt and weeds and many of the large shade trees had fallen victim to some sort of disease and had been cut down or were ready to topple over. When I asked for a refund, the camp director actually laughed at me and pointed to the small print on the brochure that stated all reservations are final. I'm pretty sure this campsite does all of its business by setting up a booth at outdoors shows and tricking people into staying there. I can't imagine anyone who comes there would come back a second time.

Now, when I find a campground I'm interested in, I do a bit more research to make sure I'm getting what I think I'm getting.

First, I call the campground and ask pointed questions to make sure they actually have the amenities I'm interested in. Next, I head to a few of the review sites there are online to see if people have posted reviews. Here are the sites I check:

RV Park Reviews (http://www.rvparkreviews.com/)

This site is mainly suited toward the RV crowd, but it has nearly 200,000 reviews on it and you can get a decent idea of what a campground is like by reading the reviews.

Campsite Photos (http://www.campsitephotos.com/)

This site can be hit or miss, but if you're lucky, you'll find a number of good photos of the current condition of the campground you're thinking of staying in. There are photos of individual campsites for many of the public campgrounds across the United States.

Trip Advisor (http://www.tripadvisor.com/) and **Yelp** (http://www.yelp.com)

These two sites offer a number of user reviews for all sorts of businesses and destinations. I've found Yelp to be the more helpful of the two when it comes to choosing a campground. It helps to keep in mind that most people don't use these sites to post glowing reviews. You will, however, get a pretty good idea of the bad experiences people have had and these sites can be a great way to judge the noise level and how strict campgrounds are about making people adhere to the rules.

In addition to checking out the reviews for a campground, I check the satellite view of the campground on Google Maps and/or Mapquest. While the images aren't completely up to date, this gives me a pretty good idea of the current condition of the campground and I can sometimes zoom in far enough to scope out individual sites.

Reserve Your Site

Planning a trip should start well in advance of the trip, especially if you're planning on camping somewhere popular that requires reservations. This is especially true if you plan on staying in a popular campground on a holiday weekend. Believe it or not, there are large numbers of people who actually enjoy camping—and they enjoy it so much they'll often make reservations a year in advance in order to get the best spots in the campsite. I'm guilty of hopping on the phone the day after we return from a trip at a particularly nice spot to reserve the spot for the next year.

The longer you wait, the less likely you are to get a spot. If you do get one, you're going to get a spot that's less than desirable. The spots that are the last to go are almost always the worst spots in the campsite. People who have been camping at the same place for years snatch up all of the good spots as soon as they become available. It's almost like waiting in line to get the best seats at a concert, except the only bands you're going to hear playing are the Crickets and the Bullfrogs.

Securing a good campsite is the key to a great trip. The best site is the one that best suits the needs of your family. You're going to need to take the following items into consideration when looking for the perfect spot:

- Do you know the area you're planning on camping in?
- Is there water nearby? If so, how close to the water do you want to be?

- Is there a designated swim area or pond? If so, where is it located?
- Where are the facilities located?
- If you have a boat, do you plan on keeping it in the water? If not, how close is the launch ramp and what kind of shape is it in?
- How busy are the roads in the campsite?
- How big of a site are you going to need?
- How close together are the campsites?
- Is there shade?
- Do you need electricity and/or running water?

If you already know the area you're camping in, life is going to be a lot easier when it comes to choosing a site. Use the knowledge you already have about the area to help you decide on the best site in the campground—and then hope it's available when you call. Always have at least 5, and preferably 10, sites picked out when you call. You don't want to have your heart set on the perfect site only to find out it's taken and have to go back to the drawing board. Creating a list of multiple sites ups your odds of getting a site the first time you call.

That's all fine and dandy if you know the area you're planning a trip to like the back of your hand, but what do you do if you have no clue what site to reserve? Don't worry; you still have options.

If you live close enough to the campsite to scout it out, a day trip to recon good sites may be in order. Plan a day at the park, a picnic or even a fishing or boating trip. It doesn't matter what you plan because your real motive is to head to the campsite and scout out the best spots.

The best spots depend on what you're looking for and are largely dependent on the age of your children. Create a list of the items the perfect spot will have in advance of scouting out the campsite, so you don't forget anything once you're there. There's nothing more frustrating than remembering you forgot to check where the boat launch was and then trying to paint a mental picture of the campground to help you remember the fine details.

Write the information down for each spot you find interesting. Better yet, write it down and snap a few pictures of the spot, so you'll be able to go back and check for yourself. I like to snap a picture of the campsite number first and then take a few pictures of the site. That way, when I see a new number, I know I'm looking at a different site.

Those who live too far away from the campground or can't make it there for one reason or another should still do their due diligence. The Internet is a great place to start. Search for the campsite online and see if there's an official website. Most campgrounds have a map online that shows the location of each spot. These are more often than not drawings that leave a lot to be desired. Picking a spot from one of these drawings is slightly better than throwing darts at a board to pick your site, but you still never know what you're going to get. You can really up your odds by heading over to Google Maps or MapQuest and comparing the hand drawn map to the satellite view of the map. The satellite view, while rarely up to date, will at least show you the terrain you're going to be camping on and how many trees are probably still going to be in each campsite.

Water Can Be Very Good or Very Bad

Spots close to the water are great if your kids are older or you have a boat you want to anchor nearby off the shore. Secure a spot by the water and you'll be able to keep a close eye on your boat. This all but eliminates the worry that lake-bound pirates—or drug addicts, but I prefer to think pirates are the problem—will sneak up to your boat at night and steal your valuables. It's rare, but it does happen. I know a guy who lost a $400 propeller off his bass boat to miscreants who crept up in the dark, unbolted it and snuck away unseen. His boat was anchored in a quiet cove, just out of view.

Another benefit of a spot near the water is the entertainment factor.

Older kids can peel their clothes off and go swimming anytime they want, as long as the campsite doesn't have a designated area to which swimming is restricted. If there is a designated swim area, securing a spot close to it will allow you to watch older kids swim while staying in the comfort of your site. Long walks to the swim area in the middle of August while the sun beats down on you aren't fun, especially when you're walking with a pack of whiny kids that won't quit asking if you're getting close.

If you have fishermen in your group, a pole or two can be set out in the morning and the evening hours to see if a fish or two can be caught for table fare. There's something to be said about catching your own food from a lake a few feet away from where you're camped out. It makes men feel like real men, and you'll hear a lot of hoots and hollers when a fish is brought to shore.

Spots close to the water do have their downsides.

I once proudly selected a waterside spot near a small tributary where I thought my family would have a great time fishing and swimming. As it turned out, drought conditions had turned the tributary into a tepid swamp, complete with giant mosquitoes and large creatures crashing through the swamp at night. The mosquitoes were so big I slapped one that landed on me and it slapped me back. I never saw one of the creatures raising the ruckus at night, but I spent the entire trip awake at night, worrying whatever it was crashing through the swamp would pay us a visit. It sounds silly now, but at 4 in the morning when I was woke up by something big crashing through dry branches in the swamp, I pictured a Sasquatch ripping through our tent, snatching up one of the kids and running off into the wilderness to raise our child as one of its own.

Waterside sites aren't so great if you have young children you're going to have to keep a constant eye on lest they end up in Davy Jones locker. Campsites near steep drop-offs into deep water are particularly troublesome because even good swimmers will have trouble climbing back to safety.

A few years back, I had the brilliant idea of keeping a lifejacket on my tiniest child so the rest of the family could enjoy a lakeside spot. She was done with the lifejacket an hour after I put it on her and spent the rest of the trip screaming and trying to Houdini her way out of the life vest. I felt horrible when I noticed the lifejacket was rubbing her skin raw underneath her arms, so I ended up taking it off and hovering over her the entire trip.

Not one of my best camping memories, but it was a valuable lesson learned. If you don't want to do a headcount every time you hear a splash, stay away from waterside sites if you have young children.

The Long Walk

Restrooms at campgrounds can be few and far between. I'm not going to sugarcoat things and tell you they're always clean. They aren't. They can be dirty and nasty, especially in campgrounds that only have a few outhouses spread throughout the campsites. These outhouses can can fill up quickly over a busy weekend. I've seen outhouses that are so full the last few people to use them had to have stood on the toilet and squatted above the pile.

Keep this in mind when choosing a campground. Good campgrounds have restrooms close by and they have enough of them to accommodate the needs of the people camping at the site, even on busy weekends. Don't be afraid to call and ask the restroom cleaning schedule at a busy campground. Restrooms that are cleaned once a day can get pretty bad in between cleanings. Any less than that and they can get downright unsanitary.

Regardless of how many restrooms or outhouses a campground has, always, and I mean always, keep a few rolls of toilet paper handy—and always check to make sure there's TP before you sit down to do your business. There's nothing worse than finishing your business only to realize there isn't a scrap of toilet paper—or any paper towels—left in the entire restroom.

Showers are often even more sparsely distributed than restrooms. Smaller campgrounds may only have a single area with warm showers, usually located somewhere near the center of the campground or close to the clubhouse.

Bring plenty of change along because some campgrounds charge for use of their showers. These campgrounds usually charge a buck or two for 10 minutes of water, so you're going to want to bring lots of change along.

One more interesting note about campground showers— I've found the proximity of the campsite to the showers roughly correlates to the number of showers that are taken by the group as a whole. The further away from the showers you are, the less showers the group is going to take. If you can't stand BO, you're going to want a site close to the showers.

While I can handle having to hop in the car to drive to the showers once a day—or once every couple of days if I've been swimming in a clean lake (that counts as bathing, right?)—what I can't handle is having to travel long distances to go to the restroom. I like to drink a cocktail or two in the evening, which means driving to a distant restroom is out of the question. Long walks through dark campgrounds while I'm trying not to pee my pants isn't my idea of fun.

Sure, you can go rogue and find a nice bush or tree to pee behind, but that isn't always possible, especially if you're staying at a crowded campground over a busy holiday weekend. The convenience of a nearby tree nearly cost a good friend of mine an indecent exposure charge. She had to pee really bad and decided to head for the nearest tree. In her distressed state, she didn't notice the nice Asian family sitting in the dark in the campsite next door—at least not until they started yelling at her for peeing in their site! She was able to talk the jovial ranger into letting her off with a warning after she sheepishly agreed to apologize to the family she'd offended, but things could have turned out much worse. As it was, she had to endure angry stares from the women in the group and raised eyebrows from the men for the rest of the trip. That, and the teenage boy wouldn't quit staring at her.

Restrooms need to be within close walking distance unless you're in a remote campsite where you can be at one with the woods. The proximity of the nearest showers are up to you.

The "Boat" Launch

"Free Boat Launch for Campers Only"

The brochure for the campsite indicated there was a free boat launch. There was only one other launch I knew of on the entire lake and it was a public launch that was a 25 mile drive around to the other side of the lake. The public launch was dirty and summertime saw it packed full of drunken wake boarders cursing and carrying on.

Once out on the water, the lake was big enough to get away from the youth partying like it was Spring Break weekend on Lake Mead, but I didn't want to expose my young children to that sort of behavior, even for a fleeting moment while backing the boat down the ramp. I have to admit I was also a little jealous of the young girls in their tiny bikinis because they made me feel more than a bit insecure about my muffin top and stretch marks. I have a recurring nightmare of my husband, balding head and all, hopping out of our boat while I'm backing it down the ramp and climbing onto one of the giant party barges. The last thing I see before he's gone forever is him dancing with two buxom blondes while a group of women barely past their teenage years cheer him on and pour water over the trio.

So, since the public launch wasn't an option due to my insecurities, I'd avoided this particular lake when it came time to camp out. That is, until I stumbled across an old brochure that had those fateful words written across the front:

"Free Boat Launch for Campers Only"

The campground looked peaceful and quiet. The pictures showed happy families hanging out and having fun. This was during my pre-site scouting days, so I picked a good-looking site from the map on the back page and called it in. I secured a spot right by the launch, which in hindsight should have been a warning sign because I'd waited until a couple weeks before out trip to call.

I bragged to anyone and everyone who would listen about how I'd figured out a way to avoid the crowded (and dangerous) launch by securing a campsite on the other side of the lake at a *campground that had its own private launch*. I bragged to my husband the whole way there, while we towed our boat hundreds of miles. I bragged right up until we got to our chosen site, within eyeshot of the "boat" launch.

When I saw the free launch for the first time, my bragging turned into a string of words usually reserved only for drivers who cut me off or go too slow in the fast lane. The so-called boat launch was a dirt launch that looked ominously like a steep staircase made of dirt and moss. There were humps and ridges large enough to take out a lower unit pocking the entire exposed surface of the launch, which dropped off ominously into what appeared to be extremely shallow water. A truck was attempting to pull a small aluminum boat out of the water and all it was doing was spinning its tires in the wet dirt. A glance out into the tepid cove revealed exposed rocks and thick vegetation, sure to stop the propeller dead in its tracks long before any boat brave enough to navigate the launch made it out of the cove—if the propeller wasn't smashed to bits on one of the barely submerged rocks first.

I marched directly to the main office where I complained about the launch. The lady behind the desk apologized and told me the launch was intended for small boats, canoes and float tubes, not full-size boats. I surmised that even the smallest of boats might have trouble with the launch and those foolish enough to launch would never make it out of the "marina." The lady offered to refund my site, so I could go elsewhere, but I relented because I knew there wouldn't be an open spot anywhere else on the lake.

Our boat sat parked alongside our campsite the entire trip, while my kids and husband forlornly looked back and forth between the launch and the boat, the boat and the launch. I finally relented and agreed it would be a good idea to head to the public launch. When we got there, there were long lines and partiers everywhere. When an impromptu wet T-shirt contest broke out on a nearby boat, I decided it was time to go, much to my husband and our teenage son's chagrin.

One more launch ramp horror story—A friend of mine camps out a lot in sites scattered around the Delta, which is an interconnected series of waterways that span thousands of miles of shoreline. He went camping one day at a site that advertised having a launch ramp that would put him dead square in some of the best fishing in the Delta.

He arrived at the campground to find a typical Delta launch. To launch his boat, he would have to maneuver a 90 degree turn to get the boat onto the steep ramp. No big surprise there, as the launch ramps on the Delta are all notoriously steep. His truck was big and strong and he had 4-wheel drive, so steep ramps weren't a problem. His wife sat in the boat as he backed it down the ramp. The boat hit the water and he started to back it in far enough to allow his wife to drive the boat off the trailer. He was halfway there when the trailer dropped abruptly out from beneath the boat with a loud thunk. The boat floated away, leaving my friend perplexed.

He shrugged his shoulders and tried to pull the trailer up the ramp to park it in the nearby lot. The wheels spun, but couldn't pull out the trailer. He locked his truck into 4-wheel drive and was rewarded with 4 spinning wheels. Placing the truck in 4 LOW had no effect. He got out and assessed the situation. Still confused, he walked back to his truck to try again when an older gentleman walked up and said, "You too, huh?" The man then explained that the concrete portion of the ramp was too short and the currents that run through the Delta had undercut the ramp, leaving a steep drop at the end of the concrete. My friend wasn't the first person to drive their trailer off the end of the ramp and probably wouldn't the last.

To make a long story short, my friend enlisted the help of the man, who attached a tow strap to his truck and used his big dually to help him pull his truck and trailer out. He then had to drive 10 miles to the next closest launch ramp to meet his wife and get his boat back on the empty trailer.

The moral of the story?

Don't assume a launch ramp is going to be in good enough shape to launch your boat from, especially if you have a larger boat. Call ahead and save yourself the time and trouble of finding out a launch isn't exactly what it's being advertised as after you've arrived at the site.

Playing in Traffic

Here's a consideration you should make that most people don't think of until after the fact. Main arteries into busy campgrounds see quite a bit of traffic, especially in the mornings and evenings as people head out for the day and come back at the end of the day.

Don't think for a second that just because the posted speed limit is 5 MPH that people will stick to it. Sure, some people will respect the posted signs, but others could care less that there are children playing within feet of the road they're speeding down. They careen down the roads carelessly, putting everyone in the campsite at risk. Everyone seems to be in a hurry, and it's rare to find someone willing to obey the posted speed limits.

Dirt roads present an even greater problem because then you've got massive amounts of dust to deal with every time someone drives by. Stay in a campsite on a dusty road in a busy campground and you and everything you brought with you will be covered in an inch thick of dust. You'll end up feeling like you're camped out in the Sahara in the middle of a dust storm.

The best sites in busy campgrounds are off the beaten path. Small loops away from main arteries into and out of the campground will give you a reprieve from the traffic and the associated dirt and dust.

Try to get a site close enough to the exit that you'll be able to get in and out in a reasonable amount of time, but realize the closer you are to the front, the more crowded the area you're camping is likely to be. This won't matter on a holiday weekend, as all the sites in the campground are likely to be full, but choosing a site that's further back in the campground on a non-prime weekend can net you a good bit of space between you and your nearest neighbor.

A Little Space, Please

Good campgrounds offer plenty of space between sites. There will be plenty of room to set up tents and spread out. The obligatory fire ring and picnic table will be far enough away from the tents that you don't have to worry about your tent going up in a blaze of melted nylon if a gust of wind hits the fire just right. Campsites in good campgrounds are designed with comfort in mind and there's plenty of space for everyone.

Bad campgrounds, on the other hand, are designed to make the owners as much money as humanly possible. The sites in this sort of campground tend to be tiny and are stacked one on top of the other. There's only room for a couple small tents or one large tent and you're left feeling crammed into your spot like a sardine in a tin.

When it comes to campgrounds like this, you have a couple options. You can avoid them completely, instead opting to seek out locations with bigger spaces where you don't feel like you're camping in a refugee camp. This isn't always an option, especially if the campsite is the only one in the area where you want to camp.

Your next option will cost you more money, but it'll at least afford you a bit of space. Instead of reserving a single tiny spot to crowd into, reserve multiple spaces next to one another. For an extra $12 to $20 an night, you'll have room to spread out and enjoy yourself, instead of having to listen to your neighbor's talk about NASCAR as they shotgun beers while sitting around their campfire.

Be careful not to underestimate the amount of space you're going to need. It's great to be able to save money by only paying for one space, but you don't want your campsite to end up too crowded. You're there to have fun, not to spend hours awake at night listening to your neighbors snore and pass gas.

Shady Acres

Camping on a hot summer day can be relaxing or it can be miserable, depending on how much shade your campsite has. A few trees can make all the difference when temperatures climb into the 90's and above.

Look for sites with large trees that will provide a canopy from the sun throughout the day. The sun rises in the east, so plan accordingly when you pick a camping spot and set up your tent. Ideally, the spot you pick will have morning sun, which will dry off your tent and warm you up a bit in the morning, and afternoon shade, so you can get out of the sun when the day starts to get hot.

Do You Need Utilities?

By utilities, I mean running water and electricity. You're going to have to make a decision as to whether you need them or not, because this will limit you as to your choices of where you can camp. Many of the nicest (and least crowded) campgrounds are off the beaten path and don't offer luxuries such as running water and electricity except for maybe in the restrooms.

For years, I felt like I had to at least have water in my campsite. I don't know why I felt this way, I just did.

Electricity in the site wasn't necessary, as long as it was close by. As long as the restrooms had an electrical outlet into which I could plug my hair dryer after a warm shower, I was happy. The problem with this line of thinking is the campgrounds that offer these amenities are the first to fill up, and they're often packed full of people the entire summer. Getting away to go camping meant fighting large crowds of people and waiting in long lines for the showers and restrooms. I wasn't really getting away, insomuch as I was changing the traffic I was stuck in. Instead of waiting on a bottlenecked freeway, the bottleneck at the campground was at the launch ramp in the mornings and the evenings.

I'm going to let you in on a little secret.

Nobody *needs* running water or electricity, especially not for a few days or even a week at a campsite. Our not-so-distant ancestors didn't have either and they got along just fine. If you can learn to go without, you'll open up a whole new world of private and peaceful campsites, far from the partyers and city folk who frequent modernized campgrounds.

If you truly need electricity, get a generator. If you need warm showers, get a solar shower. Getting away should mean truly getting away. You haven't truly gone camping until you've spent a night out under the stars, with the only sound being that of the wind whispering through the trees and the occasional cricket or two. You don't get that at a normal campground packed to the brim with weekend warriors.

First Come, First Serve

There's a new trend amongst campsites, at least in my area. They take reservations for spots, but they don't actually let you reserve a spot. What you're reserving is the right to camp in one of the spots on the campground. That way, they're guaranteed to sell out and aren't left with a handful of less than desirable spots nobody wants to reserve. Since you don't get to choose, you won't know whether you're stuck with one of the bad spots until you arrive at the campground, at which time your only choice is to stay in the bad spot or head home.

This works out fine if you're staying during a time when the campground isn't crowded. The best spots might be taken, but there will still be a number of decent spots left. You'll be able to cruise through the campsite and find a good spot with ease.

Reserve a spot in one of these campgrounds during busy times and it'll be a whole different story. Campgrounds like this tend to overbook to make sure all of the spots are filled and you might arrive to find there aren't any spots left for you to stay in. They'll feed you some excuse about people staying longer than they thought they were going to, but the end result is you being left without a place to camp. It hasn't happened to me, but I've heard from a few friends who have had exactly that happen to them. Imagine driving four hours to get to a campground only to be turned away at the gate. There's no way something like that should be allowed to happen—and it doesn't at the better campgrounds.

If you are planning on staying at one of these campgrounds or a campground that doesn't take reservations but instead works on a strict first-come first-serve basis, your best bet is to have at least one member of your party head up there early in the week to secure a spot. We usually volunteer to be the early birds because it gives us a couple days of peace and quiet before the rest of the party shows up and the fun begins. Arriving early allows you to secure a good spot before the mad rush starts.

Mondays and Tuesdays are the best days to show up. There are usually at least a handful of good spots left on Wednesday. Thursdays are hit and miss and if you show up on Friday, you're out of luck unless you happen to get lucky and show up right as someone is packing up. If you or someone in your party isn't able to show up early to procure a site, you're much better off reserving a site in a campground that lets you choose a spot when making the reservation. At least then you know where you're going to be and that you have something locked in.

Choosing a Campsite When There Are No Boundaries

Camping doesn't have to mean being shoehorned into a little site in a large campground. It doesn't have to mean listening to your neighbors party it up into the wee hours of the night while you fight the urge to scream at them to shut their mouths. On the flip side of the coin, it doesn't have to mean going to bed at a certain time out of respect for your neighbors, even though you really want to party until all hours of the night, neighbors be damned.

Wilderness areas often allow camping within their boundaries, as long as certain rules are followed. Check with your local agency to see what rules apply, if any. It may be as simple as choosing a good spot in the woods and setting up camp. It's up to you whether you want to hike a ways in order to get further away from civilization. Some of the best and most peaceful spots are found along hiking trails, but this may not be an option if you have small children.

Try to stick to established campsites in these areas when you can. These spots have been used time and time again and are often in the best areas for camping. Staying in established spots has the least impact on the environment because a new spot doesn't have to be cleared and made suitable for camping. These spots often have established tent areas, fire pits and maybe even a picnic table and a pit toilet nearby, if you're lucky enough to secure one of the good spots.

If there aren't any established spots available, look for a spot with the following features:

- **No overhead hazards.** Dead trees and cliffs with loose rocks can send deadly projectiles hurtling through your campsite. Avoid overhead hazards at all costs.
- **Flat surfaces for tents.** Bumpy or sloped ground makes for a miserable night tossing and turning while trying to get comfortable. You can somewhat alleviate the discomfort by sleeping on an air mattress, but they're prone to going flat in the middle of the night.
- **Above the waterline.** If you're staying close to the water, be it a lake, river or the beach, always choose a spot that's above the waterline. If you're staying in an area prone to flash floods, choose higher ground and stay away from creek beds. Even if there's no rain forecasted, rainfall in the mountains nearby can create flash flood conditions that can endanger your life—or get everything and everyone in your campsite wet while you scramble to move to higher ground.
- **Good drainage.** If you're unlucky enough to get caught in a freak rainstorm—which isn't all that uncommon of an occurrence in some areas, even in the middle of the summer—you're going to be miserable if you chose a campsite in the middle of a drainage basin. Water runs to the lowest point in an area and that flat depression that looked so good earlier will be the first to fill up with water in a downpour.
- **Lack of pests.** Check the area for ant hills, wasp nests and tepid water that may harbor

mosquitoes. You don't want to set up your campsite only to have to move to a different area because of a major pest infestation. Standing water and areas with tall grass should be avoided whenever possible.

- **Natural wind blocks.** Tall stands of dense trees, large boulders and thick brush can all act as wind blocks to protect you at least partially from the wind.

Here are a few more tips to help you choose the right spot:

- A single tall tree in the middle of a clearing may look like an inviting place to set up camp. This is also an inviting place for lightning to strike. You don't want to be huddled up under this tree during a lightning storm.
- Breezy areas aren't always a bad thing, as they can keep bugs to a minimum. Bees and mosquitoes can't bug you if they aren't able to fly. The less wind there is, the more bugs you're going to encounter.
- Canyons tend to be windy places. The wind will blow up the canyon during the day and down the canyon at night.
- Fog will often settle in valleys, leaving them damp and cold in the early hours of the morning.
- Snakes love deadfalls and rocky ledges. Steer clear of these areas when setting up camp.

- Watch out for poison oak, nettles and poison ivy. Touch any of these and you're in for a bad time.

Pick the right campsite and you're going to have a good time. Pick the wrong site and you're in for a miserable existence. Picking the right site in advance is one of the most important things you can do to ensure a fun and productive trip.

Triple Check Your List

I cannot stress enough the importance of creating a list of items you're going to need. If you're planning a trip, you can never start building your list too soon. As you remember items you need to take along, add them to the list.

When the big day comes rolling around and you're packing for your trip, consult the list and make sure every items gets packed into your vehicle(s) one by one. Don't cross an item off the list unless you personally see it get loaded into a vehicle. That way, you're in complete control of the list and everything that gets packed. It may sound like I'm being a bit obsessive, but kids and husbands can be a bit flippant about the items they've packed. They'll answer yes just to get you off their backs, even if they haven't actually packed into a vehicle yet. You'll cross it off the list and it'll never get packed.

Here's a sample list to get you started. You can adjust your list according to what you need:

- **Clothes.**
  - Bathing suit.
  - Coat.
  - Gloves.
  - Hats.
  - Pajamas.
  - Pants.
  - Rain gear.
  - Sandals.
  - Shirts.
  - Shoes.

- o Shorts.
- o Socks.
- o Sunglasses.
- o Sweatshirts.
- o Underwear.
- o Water shoes.
- o Diapers and wipes.
- **Toiletries.**
  - o Brush.
  - o Comb.
  - o Contact case.
  - o Contact solution.
  - o Contacts.
  - o Cosmetics.
  - o Hand sanitizer.
  - o Medications.
  - o Shampoo.
  - o Soap.
  - o Toilet paper.
  - o Toothbrush.
  - o Toothpaste.
  - o Washcloth.
  - o Wipes.
- **Toys and Games.**
  - o Balls.
  - o Bikes.
  - o Board Games/
  - o Books.
  - o Deck of cards.
  - o Water toys.
- **Food and Food-related Supplies.**

- o Aluminum foil.
- o Barbecue.
- o Bottle opener.
- o Camp stove and gas.
- o Can opener.
- o Charcoal.
- o Cutting board.
- o Ice chest.
- o Ice.
- o Ketchup.
- o Lighter fluid.
- o Lighter.
- o List of all the food and beverage items you plan on bringing.
- o Mustard.
- o Napkins.
- o Paper plates.
- o Plastic cups.
- o Plastic wrap.
- o Pots and pans.
- o Tablecloth.
- o Utensils.
- o Water.
- o Ziploc baggies.
- **Camping Gear and Miscellaneous Equipment.**
  - o Batteries.
  - o Blankets.
  - o Bungee cords.
  - o Camera.
  - o Canopy.
  - o Cell phones and chargers.

- o Chairs.
- o Firewood.
- o First aid kit.
- o Fishing bait.
- o Fishing poles.
- o Fishing tackle.
- o Flashlights.
- o Garbage bags.
- o Generator
- o Hammer.
- o Hatchet.
- o Insect repellent.
- o Lantern, mantles and fuel.
- o Maps.
- o Money.
- o Multitool.
- o Pillows.
- o Pump.
- o Rope/paracord.
- o Shovel.
- o Sleeping bags.
- o Sleeping pads/air mattresses.
- o Sunscreen.
- o Tables.
- o Tarps.
- o Tent poles.
- o Tent stakes.
- o Tents.
- o Tools.
- o Towels.
- o Two-way radios.

The list goes on and on. Keep in mind this list isn't all-inclusive. If you're bringing a boat, you're going to have to include boat-related items on the list. Those with quads or dirt bikes will have those items on the list. If you're heading into the wilderness, you're going to need more gear than if you're heading to an established campground.

Think long and hard and write down everything you're going to need. Check it all off as you put it in a vehicle and then double check your list to make sure you have everything. I'll bet you still end up forgetting *something*. As long as it isn't one of the kids, you'll probably still have a good time…

Essential Camping Gear: There's No Need to Break the Bank

Family camping trips are usually routine trips during decent weather to places that aren't generally considered dangerous. Mid-range camping gear should more than suffice, and your wallet will thank you for it. There's no real need to spend thousands of dollars on top-notch ultralight gear and sub-zero sleeping bags when you're going to be carrying your gear 10 feet from the back of your vehicle to the campsite and will be camping in the middle of summer.

You can save a lot of money on gear by waiting until the end of the season and buying your gear at one of the big sporting goods retailers like Big 5 or Dick's Sporting Goods. I've seen camping gear marked down by as much as 75% at the end of the season to get it off store shelves. These markdowns usually aren't advertised. You'll have to check store shelves regularly to get the best deals.

Another place good deals can be had is in the second-hand market. People will sometimes buy expensive gear only to realize they don't like camping one bit. Find one of these people and you'll sometimes be able to net barely-used high end gear for pennies on the dollar. Make sure you give used gear a good once over and always test it out to make sure it works. You don't want to pay for something only to get it home and find out it doesn't work.

In order to go camping, you're going to need some basic camping gear. You can add to the basic gear or upgrade it as you see fit in the future, but the items in this chapter are a must if you're planning a camping trip.

Shelter

For most family campers, a tent is the shelter of choice.

You can get a decent tent for less than a hundred bucks. I still have the first tent I purchased and it's still serviceable. I've since upgraded to a larger tent with multiple rooms, but my first 4-man tent still sees use as a loaner tent when friends and family members who don't have gear decide they want to tag along.

At a bare minimum, you're going to want a tent that shields you from the weather and wind and keeps the insects outside where they belong. It should be durable enough to where it won't rip when you look at it wrong.

The type of tent you need depends on what kind of camping you're planning on doing. There are literally hundreds, if not thousands, of different kinds of tents out there, and they all fit some sort of need. From budget tents for frugal campers to tents that put some houses to shame, there's a tent for everyone. Just remember . . . The more complicated a tent is and the more features it has, the harder it's going to be to set up.

The best tent I ever owned was one with the poles built into it. All I had to do was set it on the ground and pull the middle up and the tent basically erected itself. I used to love that tent. I'd pull it out of the bag, wait until no one was looking and pull it up, and then I'd sit around and give everyone else a hard time about how long they were taking to set up their tents. Karma finally caught up to me when one day I went to pull the tent into position and the easy-up apparatus inside fell apart. I struggled to repair it for hours while my friends laughed and cracked jokes about how slow I was. I finally had to give up and drive 40 miles to the nearest Wal-Mart, where I bought a normal tent. While it was a bit embarrassing when my tent melted down, I still miss those days of assembling a tent in mere minutes.

When choosing your first tent, bigger isn't always better. Once you've assembled a smaller tent a few times, assembling a larger tent becomes easier because most tents assemble in a similar manner. Buy a giant multiple-room tent from the get-go and you're setting yourself up for hours of struggling to read barely passable directions while you and your husband bicker about which pole is pole A and whether or not you're inserting it into hole D or hole E.

Buy the smallest tent that will accommodate your needs to get started and you'll have a much easier time setting it up.

The multiple room tents are nice, but they tend to be pricey. If you have young kids you want sleeping in the same tent, they'll get the job done, but you better make sure your site can accommodate a monster-sized tent. Now that my kids are older, I prefer having two separate tents, so my husband and I are afforded at least a modicum of privacy. Tents are thin and as long as we set the kids' tent up nearby we can hear everything they're up to.

There are a number of features you're going to have to know about before you go shopping for a tent. Here they are, in no particular order.

All tents come with a capacity rating that tells you how many people can fit in the tent. I've found this capacity rating will leave you stacked like cordwood if you try to fit the maximum amount of people the tent is rated for into it. A tent that's rated for 4 people can indeed fit 4 people, but it had better be 4 people that really like one another. You're much better off cutting the maximum capacity in half. 2 people are going to be much more comfortable in a tent rated for 4.

If you're planning on camping in hot weather, you're going to want a tent with plenty of ventilation. Look for tents with screened windows and doors, so you'll be able to ventilate your tent without inviting every insect in the campsite inside.

Lighter colored tents reflect the rays of the sun and will be cooler than darker tents. Darker colored tents are preferable in cool weather because they absorb the rays of the sun and will keep the tent warmer inside.

You're going to have to consider the type of weather you're likely to face when purchasing a tent. Some tents are only designed to withstand 20 MPH winds, which is fine if you're in an area that doesn't see much wind. Take the same tent to a windy desert campsite and you might find yourself sleeping in the car when the tent blows over in the middle of the night. As far as rain-proofing your tent goes, most tents come with a rain fly that can be placed over the tent to keep water out. This piece can be removed to gain valuable ventilation when the weather is nice. Get caught without one in a rain storm and you're liable to end up soaked.

You're going to want *tub flooring*, which is essentially a tarp that's built into the floor of the tent. This type of flooring has no seams and usually extends half a foot up the side of the tent all the way around. This will keep ground water out and will make for a much more comfortable experience in wet conditions.

Even with tub flooring, you're going to want a tarp to place under your tent to keep it from coming in direct contact with the ground. The tarp provides an extra layer of protection against rips and tears and keeps ground water from evaporating up into your tent. If you're expecting rain, be sure to fold the edges of the tarp up under the tent or you can create a pool of water that'll sit below your tent at the lowest point of the tarp.

Spend a little extra and go with *ripstop nylon fabric* if you can afford it. This type of fabric is much more durable than the thin nylon the cheapest tents are made of. I've seen cheaper tents rip the first time someone falls into or leans against them. You aren't going to save money by having to replace your tent every time someone is a little rough with it. The ripstop nylon will withstand the rigors of camping and is the better deal over the long run.

Keep your poles in the same bag as your tent or figure out a way to attach the pole bag to your tent bag. Keeping them together helps ensure you don't forget the poles, rendering your expensive tent useless. It never fails that the trip you forget the poles on will be the one where you're hundreds of miles away from the nearest store.

The same thing goes for tent stakes. I keep an extra set of stakes in the box I have my camp stove in. That way I'll always have extra stakes on-hand. A bent or broken stake can make setting up your tent very difficult.

Tent Types

The first time I went tent shopping, I was floored by the sheer number of tent varieties I found on store shelves. I didn't know a ridge tent from a dome tent and had no clue what type of tent would best fit my needs. Luckily, I came across a nice gentleman at a local big box retailer who was more than happy to explain the various types of tents to me. Had I not run into this helpful man, I might still be in the store trying to figure out what tent to buy.

Here's a quick primer on the various tents you may come across:

Dome tent. Dome tents are a popular tent type. They have bendable poles that are usually attached to the outside of the tent. As the poles are inserted and bent, the tent forms into a dome shape. Smaller dome tents don't use a lot of poles and are relatively stable. Larger dome tents require more poles to stay stable and can be a hassle to set up.

Family tents. Huge tents designed to fit the whole family are known as family tents. They run the gamut from heavy-duty, sturdy tents to flimsy inexpensive tents that fall apart if you stand outside and blow on them. Expect to pay through the nose for a good family tent. Also expect to have to search far and wide for campsites into which you can squeeze one of these behemoths.

Frame tents. While dome tents use bendable poles, frame tents use poles that are rigid and sturdy. Frame tend to be roomy and stable, but they're tougher to set up than their lightweight counterparts.

Geodesic tent. These tents are designed to withstand seriously bad weather conditions. They tend to be expensive and are overkill for family camping trips—

unless you plan on taking your family on a trip to scale Mount Everest.

Instant-up tents. Also known as *quick-pitch tents*, instant-up tents are the easiest tents of all to set up. All you have to do is push or pull them in the right diection and they pretty much set themselves up. They're decent tents for fair-weather camping, but don't hold up well in inclement weather.

Ridge tent. This is the classic tent. It's a triangle-shaped tent that usually has a cross-pole for added support. They come in a number of sizes and are easy to set up and take down. The biggest downside to ridge tents is their height. They work great if you don't mind having to hunch over while walking around inside of one. They're great for sleeping in, but aren't a good choice if you plan on spending a lot of time in your tent.

Sleeping Bags

To be completely honest, you can get away with using blankets on summertime camping trips to areas where the weather is nice. Many people do, but as soon as the weather turns cold in the evenings, they wish they would have spent the money to buy sleeping bags.

The amount of money you have to put out for a good sleeping bag depends on the kind of weather you want to be able to use it in. Generally speaking, bags capable of keeping you warm in colder temperatures cost more than bags designed for fair weather use. Every sleeping bag sold has a temperature rating that's supposed to be the lowest temperature the bag is capable of handling. Keep in mind that this is an arbitrary number put out there by the manufacturer and there are no standards by which all bags are judged. The temperature ratings will get you in the right ballpark, but quality and warmth will vary from manufacturer to manufacturer amongst bags that have the same rating.

Manufacturers tend to overestimate their ratings. What this means is a bag rated for 30 degrees F rarely keeps you warm when temperatures dip that low. If you think you're going to experience temperatures near the minimum rating, you'd probably be better served getting a bag rated for lower temperatures.

Summer bags are designed to keep you warm down to about 30 degrees F, but you're not going to be comfortable if the temperatures drop that low. Summer bags are great in warm weather because they can be unzipped and used as blankets when temperatures are so high you don't want to be stuffed into a warmer bag.

Get caught in temperatures below 30 degrees F and you're going to be miserable trying to tough it out in a summer bag. *Three-season bags* are designed to be used in the spring and fall as well as the summer and are good down to around 15 degrees F. *Winter bags* are going to be required if you plan on camping in cooler weather than that (BRRR!). They're bigger, warmer bags, some of which are designed to keep you warm when the temperatures drop well below 0.

All sleeping bags come with a temperature rating. This rating assumes you're sleeping on a pad. Sleep on the ground and you can throw the ratings out the window. You'll be a lot colder if you don't have a pad between you and the ground.

When you go to buy a bag, don't buy the lowest temperature rating you can afford just because you can afford it. If you buy a sleeping bag rated for sub-zero temperatures and try to sleep in it on a 60 degree night, you're going to be way too hot. Get a bag rated for the weather you're most likely to face. Those planning on camping in drastically different temperatures will be best served by buying multiple bags.

If you plan on camping in cold weather, there are a few features that are nice to have. *Hoods* can be wrapped around your head and tightened to keep drafts out. *Draft collars* are designed to keep drafts away from your neck. *Draft tubes* wrap around the entire bag and are designed to keep cold drafts from entering through the zipper.

Look for a store near you that has a number of bags you can try out. Climb into the bag and feel how warm it feels in the store. You might even be able to talk the clerk into letting you take the bag outside to try it if the weather is cold. While you're at it, test the zippers to make sure they don't get snagged when you're completely zipping and unzipping the bag. Snaggy zippers can be a real pain when you're camping and a good bag is built to minimize snags.

Bag Shapes

There are a handful of bag shapes you can buy. Here they are, with a brief description of each:

Rectangular: These bags are usually lower-end bags designed with the budget camper in mind. They aren't particularly warm or efficient, but might be suitable if you only plan on taking fair-weather camping trips.

Mummy: These bags are designed to wrap you up in a tight cocoon and keep you warm. They're wide at the top and narrow at the bottom in order to ensure the heat generated by your body stays close to your body. They're great for warmth, but not so good if you toss and turn a lot because they're rather restrictive.

Alternative cuts: These bags fall somewhere between rectangular and mummy. They're warmer than rectangular cut bags and give you more leg room than the mummy bags. They work well and bags are available for pretty much any temperature you'd reasonably want to take your family camping in.

Fill Materials: It's What's On the Inside that Counts

The fill material of your sleeping bag largely determines the quality of the bag. There are 2 basic choices when it comes to fill materials. *Down filling*, which is made from the fluffy under-feathers of waterfowl like ducks and geese, and *synthetic filling*, which is made from man-made materials.

Both materials have their pros and cons.

Down is generally considered a higher quality fill material than synthetic stuffing. It's warmer and lighter than synthetic filling and it holds up better over time. Down wicks moisture away from the body as you sweat at night, which goes a long way toward keeping you comfortable. Most synthetic materials try to mimic the properties of down, but fall well short of the mark.

Don't run out and buy a down sleeping bag just yet. There are some issues you need to be aware of. The biggest downside to down sleeping bags is the price. They're expensive because the down has to be harvested from birds and can't be recreated in a factory setting. Because down is a product from nature, down bags have to be cleaned using gentle cleansing products designed to clean down without destroying it.

All down is not equal.

High-quality down has a higher *loft rating*, which is the amount of space in cubic inches one ounce of down will take up when placed in a beaker. Lower-quality down is rated around 600, while the best stuff approaches 900. The loftier the down, the cozier you're going to be when temperatures dip down close to what the bag is rated for.

Synthetic material-filled sleeping bags are less expensive than those filled with down because synthetic filling can be created in a factory setting in large amounts. If you plan on camping in wet conditions, synthetic filling may be the better choice because it dries quickly and doesn't become matted like down. Synthetic bags will keep you warm when there's a lot of moisture present. Down bags won't. Synthetic bags are also a good choice for those allergic to down because they won't cause an allergic reaction.

Synthetic bags are heavier than down bags, which isn't a big deal for those who only plan on moving their sleeping bag from a vehicle to a nearby campsite. If you plan on backpacking, this extra weight could be an issue. Synthetic filling also isn't as durable as down and tends to degrade over time. If you're looking to buy one bag you can keep for a lifetime, down is probably the better choice.

When it comes to synthetic vs. down filling, there isn't a clear correct choice. If you're a weekend warrior looking to camp on a weekend here and there during the summer, the extra cost of a down sleeping bag may not be worth it. On the other hand, if you're looking to get a quality sleeping bag that'll give you the most bang for your buck, down is a good choice—as long as it doesn't wet.

Storing Your Sleeping Bag

At the end of a camping trip it's all too easy to stuff your sleeping bag in the little stuff sack it came with and toss it in the garage and forget about it until the next trip. That's what most people do, and I've been guilty of it myself in the past.

When you store your bag stuffed into a small stuff bag, you're drastically shortening the life of the bag. Both down and synthetic bags should be removed from the stuff sack when you get home and either placed into a large pillowcase that gives them room to breathe or spread out and stored somewhere they can be left open.

The longer you leave your sleeping bag stuffed into a stuff sack, the less likely it becomes the bag will return to normal when you remove it from the sack. The stuffing breaks down at a much faster rate when it's stored compressed as opposed to loose, so store your bag decompressed to prolong its life.

Sleeping Pads

While not having an air mattress or sleeping pad isn't going to kill you, it can be the difference between tossing and turning all night and getting a good night's sleep. Both air mattresses and sleeping pads provide insulation from the ground and are an added layer or protection between your body and the sticks and stones you missed when you cleared a place for your tent.

I don't want to sound like the princess from *The Princess and the Pea* here, but sleeping on ground with even a few sticks and rocks under the tent can be extremely uncomfortable if you don't use an air mattress or sleeping pad. Add in this extra layer and you won't feel all but the biggest of sticks and stones.

Air mattresses and air pads feature compartments that are filled with air. *Air pads* are lightweight pads that usually use both foam and air for insulation. They're lighter than *air mattresses*, which are thick air-filled mattresses that are as close to a real mattress as you're going to get. They tend to be heavy and bulky and typically require use of a pump to fill them, but that really isn't an issue for most family camping trips. The downside to air pads and mattresses is they aren't very durable and can be punctured. The upside is they're easy to repair, as long as you have a repair kit on hand.

If you do buy an air mattress or air pad, be sure to invest in a good one. I've bought a few of the cheaper ones and every one I've bought loses air throughout the night. Unless you want to wake up at three in the morning and wake up everyone around you when you turn on the pump to refill your mattress, you're going to want to invest in a quality air mattress that doesn't lose air when you lay on it.

Foam pads are a lightweight and easy option for those who don't want to deal with the hassle of filling and deflating air-filled pads. They're inexpensive and durable, but don't provide as much protection as the larger air mattresses do—when they're filled all the way up. If you decide to go with a foam pad, the thicker pads are much more comfortable. A 3" to 4" pad should provide plenty of protection and insulation.

Let There Be Light

When the sun goes down, campsites tend to get dark. Really dark. So dark you can't see your nose in front of your face. I was shocked at how dark things got when the sun went down the first time I camped out under a waning moon.

To combat the darkness, you're going to need several types of lights.

The first light you're going to want is some sort of lantern, which can be used to light up the entire campsite or the inside of your tent, whichever you prefer. Camping lanterns fall into two basic classes: fuel lanterns and electric lanterns. Fuel lanterns are classic lanterns that run off of some sort of fuel, while electric lanterns use batteries or have to be plugged in to work.

Fuel Lanterns

Fuel lanterns are available that utilize a number of different fuels:

Butane. Butane lanterns use butane canisters and are one of the easier lanterns to use. Self-igniting lanterns are available, but they tend to be a bit unreliable, so make sure you have a lighter or matches available. Butane doesn't work well when the weather drops below 40 degrees F or at high altitudes, so plan accordingly.

Gas. These lanterns burn bright, but tend to be expensive and use an actual flame to provide light. Gas lanterns aren't the best choice for families with small children because gas canisters can cause fires if they're knocked over. Refilling gas lanterns can also be problematic because gas is extremely flammable.

Kerosene. Kerosene lanterns are durable and heavy. They can handle a bit more abuse than other types of fuel lanterns, but the added weight makes them unwieldy and difficult to move around.

Propane. Canisters of propane are the typical fuel source for propane lanterns, which burn bright and are lightweight and easy to use.

There are considerations you have to make when using fuel lanterns. The first is the fact that they pretty much all use glass globes. Some of the thinner glass globes break if you so much as look at them wrong, so they need to be placed somewhere they won't get knocked over. Fuel lanterns create carbon monoxide as they burn, so they aren't a good choice for inside the tent. They also create heat and the glass globes can heat up enough to burn the hands of young children and careless adults, so plan accordingly.

Many fuel lanterns require the use of *mantles*, which are small pieces of cloth that light up brightly to increase the amount of light generated by the fuel as it burns. While they're generally easy to install and use, they're one more thing you have to remember when it comes time to pack for a camping trip.

Electric Lanterns

Unless you plan on only camping in sites with electrical hookups or you plan on having a generator with you, electric lanterns that have to be plugged in to work aren't a good choice. Battery-powered lanterns are the better choice for camping, provided you have ample amounts of batteries on-hand. You're also going to want to keep an extra bulb or two.

If you decide to use a battery-powered lantern, be aware that they aren't as bright as fuel lanterns. They are safer for children to use, so they may be a good choice when you have small children around. They're also a good choice for inside the tent because they don't produce dangerous gases as they create light.

I like to keep a combination of battery- and fuel-powered lanterns on-hand while camping. A fuel-powered lantern is used to light up the campsite because it burns brighter and lasts a long time. When we have young children around, we hang the lantern up high, so it's out of reach.

Several small battery-powered lanterns are also kept on-hand. We use them when we want to light our way when we walk around the campground and to light up our tents for short periods of time. This allows us to take advantage of the best qualities of both battery and fuel lanterns.

Flashlights

In addition to a lantern or two, you're going to want flashlights you can use while camping. Choosing a flashlight for camping can be a difficult decision because there are so many different types of flashlights available.

The first decision you're going to have to make is the type of bulb(s) you want your flashlight to have.

LED bulbs are extremely durable, long-lasting bulbs that can last as long as 100,000 hours before burning out. Some of the better lights feature low-energy bulbs that extend battery life out into the hundreds of hours. The long bulb and battery life comes at the cost of power, as LED bulbs tend not to be as powerful as incandescent bulbs. They work great for short distances, but don't reach out as far as the brighter bulbs.

Incandescent bulbs use a heated filament to produce light. They aren't as efficient as LED lights and require more power, but they're brighter as a result. If you want a light that is bright and can light up a large swath in front of you, an incandescent light is a good choice. Lights that have gases like xenon or halogen added to the light chamber are even brighter, but will cost you more money.

I keep an expensive incandescent flashlight with my camping gear for nighttime hikes and walks through the campsite to the restroom after dark. I also keep a couple of the less-expensive LED lights around for the kids to play with. The LED lights are more durable and I don't have to worry about them getting broken like I would if the kids were playing with the good flashlight.

I also keep a couple *headlamps*, which are flashlights attached to headbands. They come in handy when I need to do something in the dark that requires both hands.

Keeping It Cool: The Ice Chest

Unless you want to drink warm beverages and live on a diet of chips and crackers, you're going to need some sort of ice chest or cooler. The type and size of cooler you can get largely depends on how much room you have in the vehicle you're planning on trying to pack it into. No matter the type, you need your cooler to do one thing—keep your food and drinks cold until you want to consume them. All ice chests are not created equally, so it's important you know what you're getting in order to avoid nasty surprises later on down the road.

While those foam ice chests sitting on top of the adult beverage coolers in your local supermarket work great for keeping beer cold in a pinch, you aren't going to want to try to use one of them for a camping trip. You want a cooler with insulation that'll keep things cold for as long as possible. Styrofoam coolers aren't durable enough to withstand the rigors camping and ice placed in these coolers melts quickly, so they're rarely used on camping trips. The money you save buying a cheap cooler will be spent replacing rapidly melting ice or buying new food because the food you have went bad after the ice melted.

Plastic or metal ice chests are much better choices for camping, as they're more insulated and can withstand a bit of abuse. Metal coolers are the strongest, but they're also the heaviest and are more expensive than plastic coolers. Since plastic is lighter, you can find huge plastic ice chests capable of holding a large amount of food and drinks. If you buy a huge cooler, make sure you get one with wheels and strong handles you can use to lift it when it's full of food and ice.

Coolers are rated by both size and the number of days ice is supposed to last on a 90 degree F day. Cooler size is almost always measured in quarts. Sizes range from small coolers designed to hold a handful of sodas or a single lunch to humongous coolers that hold 150 quarts or more. For a family of 4, a 25 to 50 quart ice chest should be sufficient to hold food and an additional 25 quart chest can be used for drinks. Separate the food and drinks into separate ice chests whenever possible because the drink ice chest will be constantly open throughout the day. You want to keep your food ice chest closed except for when you need food from it in order to ensure the food stays chilled and fresh.

The days rating you choose is up to you, but you want at least a 3-day ice chest. Keep in mind that this is an optimistic estimate that doesn't factor in opening the ice chest multiple times throughout the day. A 5-day chest will usually get you through 2 to 3 days without having to replace the ice, depending on how many times the chest is opened and how long it's left open for.

Tips for Keeping Things Cold

There's nothing more frustrating than opening an ice chest to find all of the ice has melted and temperatures are rising. Following Murphy's Law, this usually happens at the most inconvenient of times.

The following tips should help you get the most from your ice chest . . . and the ice in it. Block ice lasts longer and is more effective than crushed ice. The solid mass of ice has less air pockets than crushed ice, so less of the total surface of the ice is exposed to the air.

The following tips will help you keep things colder in your ice chest:

- **Don't leave the lid open for long periods of time.** Decide what you want in advance, get in and get it quick.
- **Fill your icebox as full as possible.** The fuller the cooler, the longer it will take for ice to melt.
- **Freeze all the items you're able to freeze in advance before the trip.** They'll stay frozen and keep things cool for at least part of the trip.
- **If you're making your own ice, add a bit of salt to the water before freezing it.** This will lower the freezing temperature of the ice and will make the ice colder.
- **Items that can't be frozen should at least be cooled in the fridge before being placed in the chest.** Warm items will begin to melt ice on contact.
- **It's best to freeze ice packs or jugs of water for the ice chest you're planning on keeping your food in.** This will prevent water from getting into your food and contaminating both the food and the ice water.
- **Temperatures are coolest at the bottom of the ice chest, so pack meats and other delicate foods near the bottom.**
- **Throw a blanket over the cooler to insulate it from the sun.** Keep it in the shade whenever possible.

First Aid: What You Need in Your Kit

The size of first aid kit you need largely depends on where you plan on camping. If you plan on camping in developed sites close to society, a small kit will usually suffice. Any major first aid needs can be addressed by medical professionals that are a phone call away. On the other hand, if you plan on camping miles away from the nearest medical professional, you're going to need a much larger kit designed with the fact in mind that you might have to provide medical care for a major injury until you can get the injured person to the hospital.

It's up to you to decide how big of a kit you're going to need, but I'll tell you this. In a crisis situation, nobody has ever complained about having too much by way of first aid supplies. On the other hand, not having enough could result in major complications or even death if proper care isn't provided within a reasonable amount of time.

Once you decide what you need, it's time to learn how to use the stuff you have.

While survival first aid is beyond the scope of this book, you're going to want to know a thing or two about applying at least basic first aid while camping. The biggest and baddest first aid kit in the world isn't any good without the knowledge of how to use it. At the very least, read through a first aid field guide like *Medicine for the Outdoors: The Essential Guide to First Aid and Medical Emergency* a couple times before your trip and keep it handy in case you need it.

Here are some of the items you might want to include in your first aid kit:

- Alcohol cleansing pads.
- Allergy medicine.
- Aloe vera gel.
- Antacid.
- Antibacterial cream.
- Antibacterial wipes.
- Anti-diarrheal medications.
- Antihistamine.
- Assorted adhesive bandages.
- Assorted fabric bandages.
- Assorted sizes of safety pins.
- Bug bite relief ointments.
- Butterfly bandages.
- Cotton balls.
- Duct tape.
- EpiPen (for allergic reactions).
- Eye drops.
- Eye pads.
- Gauze.
- Hand sanitizer.
- Hemostatic gauze.
- Hydrogen peroxide.
- Insect repellent.
- Lip balm.
- Medical tape.
- Mirror.
- Moleskin.

- Multitool.
- Needle and thread.
- Pain-relief medication.
- Prescription medications.
- Q-tips.
- Rehydration salts.
- Scissors.
- Space blanket.
- Splints.
- Sunscreen.
- Superglue.
- Surgical gloves.
- Thermometer.
- Tweezers.
- Water purification tablets.
- Wire cutters.

Supplies should be kept in an airtight, waterproof container. Be sure to swap out medications and other perishable items before they reach the end of their useful lives.

Dress for Success

The way you dress while camping will largely determine how comfortable you are. By choosing the right clothing for the trip, you'll ensure you're always as comfortable as possible. The correct clothing will protect you from the elements without leaving you too hot or too cold. While you're going to want to prepare for any type of weather, you also want to pack light and avoid bringing a bunch of clothing items you aren't going to need.

There's a fine line between packing smart and filling bag after bag with clothing you aren't going to use, so where do you draw the line? This largely depends on where you're planning on camping and what you're planning on doing while you're there. A summer camping trip to the beach is going to require packing different clothing items than a fall camping trip in the mountains. A fishing trip to a foothill lake in the spring will require different clothing items than a trip to the same lake in the middle of summer for water skiing and tubing.

What I like to do is break clothing items up into classes based on how likely I am to need them. The classes I use are:

- **Likely to need.**
- **Might need.**
- **Probably won't need.**

Simple enough. There's no need to overcomplicate things with more than three classes. Now, consider the location you're traveling to and break your clothing up into one of the three categories.

Let's look at an example using a camping trip to the mountains in the middle of the summer. The weather is likely to be warm during the day and cool at night. There's always the possibility of a summer storm, which can come on in a hurry and might dump quite a bit of rain in a short period of time.

Here's an example of how I'd break my clothing items down for a trip to the mountains in the summer:

Likely to need:
Shorts, sandals, tank tops, T-shirts, light sweatshirts, pants, sweatpants, tennis shoes, baseball cap.

Might need:
Heavier sweatshirts, light jackets, rain gear.

Unlikely to need:
Heavy winter clothing, snowshoes, gloves, beanie.

I start by packing everything I have on the likely to need list and as much as I can on the might need list. This covers the situations you're most likely to be faced with.

Then I take a look at the unlikely to need list and assess how likely the items I've placed on the list are. Heavy winter clothing probably isn't going to be needed in the summer in the mountains. If it gets too cold, we could add layers from the might need list and still stay warm. There's no real need to pack heavy winter clothing and snowshoes.

Even if it were to snow, it would probably only be a light dusting that melted off quickly.

On the other hand, a trip to the mountains in the fall would require a much different set of clothing. Here's how I would break things down for a fall camping trip:

Likely to need:
Heavier sweatshirts, light jackets, rain gear, pants, beanie.

Might need:
Heavy winter clothing, snowshoes, sweatpants, T-shirts, light sweatshirts, tennis shoes, gloves, baseball cap.

Unlikely to need:
Shorts, sandals, tank tops.

As you can see, the categories of most of the clothing items have changed. I'd go heavy on everything in the likely to need and might need categories. I'd also toss in a pair of shorts and a tank top or two just in case we experienced unseasonably warm weather. The weather could be cool or warm during the day and will likely be cold at night. Depending on how late in the season the trip is planned for, snow could be a real possibility, so I'd have to plan accordingly.

Bring warm clothes to an area that's likely to be cool, but don't forget to pack at least a few lighter items. You never know when you'll be faced with an unseasonably warm day, and you're going to regret not having something light to wear if this happens. What you pack will largely depend on how cool the weather could potentially get. Pack mostly light clothes when you're going to an area that's likely to be warm, but don't skimp on the warmer clothing items. Some areas can really cool off in the evenings and you're going to want to be able to warm up a bit if you need to.

I once went camping in the high desert with a group of friends in the middle of summer. I told them the weather could get cold at night and told them to pack accordingly. The first night was fairly cold and I was glad I packed my long johns. I was snug as a bug and didn't even notice the cold until I got up in the morning. I was having my morning coffee when two of friends we were camping with pulled up in their car. They'd been so cold during the night, they were actually worried about freezing to death. They'd grabbed their wallets and car keys around 1 in the morning and drove 30 miles to the nearest motel where they spent the night, all while I was nice and cozy in my tent in my long johns and sleeping bag. I was sleeping so deeply, I hadn't even heard them leave.

It was then and there that I realized the importance of having the right clothing and gear for the situation. Their trip was ruined and they headed home that day. We stayed an additional 3 days and had a blast—and hardly noticed the cold nights.

The Art of Layering

If you aren't sure what the weather is going to be like, you're going to have to pack a little bit of everything. The beaches in my area have wildly fluctuating temperatures, even in the middle of summer. One day it'll be 100 degrees with blazing sun and a day later it'll be foggy and in the 50's during the day with nighttime temperatures creeping down to the 40's.

When I'm headed out on a trip like this, where the weather could be bone-chilling cold or blistering hot, I like to pack clothing that can be added in layers based on how hot or cold the weather turns out to be.

Start off with the *under layer*, which is your underwear and undershirt. A wicking undershirt can work wonders on both hot and cold day. It'll keep you insulated in the cold and will wick away sweat when it's hot, keeping you more comfortable when the temperature swings in either direction. Avoid cotton clothes in this layer if the weather is likely to turn cold and wet because it holds moisture close to your skin.

Middle layer clothes are the clothes you normally wear when the weather is moderate or warm. Clothes worn in this layer include T-shirts, blouses, pants, shorts and long sleeve shirts. This layer may be all you need on a nice day or when the weather turns warm, but you're going to be hurting if the weather turns cold and all you have packed are under and middle layer clothes.

Cool weather clothes go over the top of middle layer clothes when the weather turns cool, but not excessively cold. Clothing for this layer includes light jackets, sweatshirts, vests, light rain gear, sweatpants and windbreakers. This layer will protect you from moderately cool weather, but will be inadequate if the weather turns nasty.

Winter layer clothes are the last layer of clothing to go on as the weather worsens. This layer is your last line of defense against the cold and should be on par with the worst weather you can reasonably expect. Wool caps, snow gloves, heavy rain gear, thick winter jackets and snow pants are all winter layer clothing. If the weather turns cold enough to need this gear for any extended period of time, most families will call the trip and head for warmer pastures. It's still important to have winter layer clothes on hand if there's the potential for nasty weather because it can be the difference between life and death if you get stranded.

The nice thing about packing clothes you can layer is you're ready for anything. You can strip down to shorts and a tank top if the weather is warm and you can add layers if it starts to cool down as evening approaches. Pack more clothing for the type of weather you're expecting, but keep items from each of the 4 layers on hand. That way, you'll be ready for pretty much anything Mother Nature decides to throw at you. Go camping enough and you'll experience snow in the summer and sunny days in the winter and you'll be glad you have layers of clothing you can add to and remove from your body as needed.

Family Camping Safety

A family camping trip is supposed to be an enjoyable experience for the entire family. With the fun comes the responsibility of camping safely and making sure everyone that goes camping comes back in one piece. There are some common camping dangers you need to be aware of and keep an eye out for both while in your campsite and while roaming around exploring the area you're camped out in.

Beat the Heat

The most common camping injuries come about as a result of the sun. Hot days can result in heat exhaustion, especially in the elderly and young children who haven't yet developed the full ability to sweat to cool themselves off. Keep trips that involve being exposed to the sun short for the more vulnerable members of your family and try to limit exerting activities to early in the day and late in the evening. Spend time back at the campsite in the shade during the heat of the day.

Wearing light, loose fitting clothing made of breathable materials can help cool you down in the heat. Drink plenty of water. Drinking other liquids containing caffeine, sugar or alcohol can actually worsen the effects of the sun on the body. Monitor everyone in your party closely for signs of distress, as heat stroke can kill a person who isn't properly treated.

Learn to recognize the signs of heat stress. The following signs are indicative of heat stress. Get anyone showing any of these signs out of the sun and cool them down:

- Clamming skin.
- Confusion.
- Cramping.
- Dizziness.
- Elevated body temperature.
- Experiencing chills.
- Fatigue.
- Flushing.

- Hallucinations.
- Headache.
- Heat rash.
- Lack of sweat.
- Nausea.
- Profuse sweating.
- Rapid breathing.
- Shaking.
- Slurred speech.
- Weakness.

If you suspect a member of your party is suffering from heat stroke, seek immediate medical attention. Death and permanent disability can result if heat stroke is left untreated.

Sunburn is another danger associated with the sun.

While most sunburns are first degree burns that are only mildly irritating and go away after a couple days, repeatedly allowing the skin to burn can result in complications like skin cancer, wrinkles and premature aging later on down the road.

Fair skin is more susceptible to sunburns and second degree burning can occur if the skin is exposed to the rays of the sun for long periods of time. Badly burnt skin will be extremely painful to the touch and blisters may form. Bad sunburns can require medical attention, especially if sun poisoning takes place, which is a condition in which the entire body reacts to the sunburn. Chills, vomiting and extreme nausea can all come about as a result of a bad sunburn.

Avoid sunburns by staying out of the sun. When this isn't possible, wear protective clothing, a hat and sunglasses and cover exposed areas with broad-spectrum sunblock that blocks both UVA and UVB rays. Reapply it regularly, especially if you're swimming or sweating.

Be aware you can get sunburnt even on a cloudy day. Some of the rays of sun make it through cloud cover, so you're still going to want to protect yourself.

Avoid Campsite Hazards

Camping is a pastime that's generally regarded as safe, but there are some considerations that must be made that you probably don't have to worry about when your kids are playing in the backyard at home.

Campgrounds are generally kept clean because they largely rely on repeat business from people who return to the campground year after year. Dirty campgrounds don't get repeat customers and will soon find themselves empty, save but the few people who couldn't find spots somewhere else. You still have to keep in mind that there have been large numbers of people camping in most sites before you got there and they may have left something behind you don't want your kids playing with. Before setting up your tent, do a quick sweep of the campsite and look for dangerous items like broken glass, animal (or human) feces, razor blades, dirty napkins or diapers and needles. I rarely find anything dangerous, but when I do I'm glad I did the scan.

It's also a good idea to scan the area for hazardous wildlife like fire ants and bees. Ticks are of concern because they can be carriers of Lyme disease. Check your children and pets closely for ticks. If a tick is found, remove it immediately and monitor the child for signs of Lyme disease.

If you're in an area bears frequent, be aware they will forage for fruit and other food items left accessible in the site. Raccoons will also raid your site and tear into food that's been left out. You haven't seen a mess until you've seen a campsite raided by raccoons. Keep your food in containers animals can't get into, store it in your car or hang it out of reach. When camping somewhere there might be large animals roaming around, keep your kids close to your site, so they won't become a tasty snack.

Teach your kids well in advance of the trip that any wildlife they see is to be appreciated from a distance, but never approached without the approval of an adult. Kids often think it's OK to feed small wild animals from their hands. This is a good way to get a nasty bite if they suddenly startle the animal. Wild animals can carry diseases and may harbor ticks and fleas. Let your kids know they need to stop and call for an adult anytime they see a wild animal near the campsite. I was once at a campsite where a kid brought a pocketful of baby rattlesnakes back to camp. How he wasn't bitten, I'll never know, but his parents nearly had a heart attack when he started pulling them from his pocket.

Hazardous plants like poison oak, poison ivy and sumac should be identified and avoided. Show your kids what the plants look like in advance and let them know the result of touching these plants. If they aren't sure what a plant is, they should avoid it at all costs. They should also be discouraged from eating any berries, mushrooms or other plants they find they think might be edible. If they do come in contact with an irritating plant, wash their skin immediately and apply calamine lotion to the affected area. Scratching the itching area can cause the infection to spread, so discourage rubbing and scratching.

You might be concerned with all the dirt and germs floating about, but I've generally found they aren't much of a concern. Let your kids know they need to stay away from any dead animals or piles of animal droppings they may happen across. Have them wash their hands with antibacterial soap prior to mealtime and they should be good to go.

Of greater concern is them drinking water from natural sources. While they probably aren't going to get sick from accidentally ingesting a bit of water from the lake or swimming pond, they need to know that they should never drink water from a natural source, no matter how clean it looks. Parasites like giardia are invisible to the naked eye and can cause extreme gastrointestinal distress if consumed.

In the event an emergency does occur, stay calm and don't panic. Avoid making rash decisions based on fear and instead assess the situation and try to make the right decision.

Set Clear Boundaries

This section is going to be short, but the information in it is absolutely critical to ensuring your children stay safe. Setting boundaries in a campground which children aren't allowed to cross without permission will help keep kids from wandering too far away and getting lost.

Younger children and toddlers should be confined to the campsite. Discourage them from wandering into the street and let them know they aren't allowed to approach the campfire or lantern without an adult in tow.

Older children can be confined to whatever boundaries you see fit, but should never be let completely out of sight. It's too easy for even a mature child to wander off and get lost while they're traipsing about checking out anything that piques their interest. They should also be kept out of other occupied campsites, unless they have both the permission of the people camping in the site and your permission to go hang out there.

Teenagers can be allowed a bit more freedom, but again, it's easy for a teenager to get lost if allowed to wander too far away from camp. You should still set clear boundaries which the teenagers in your group aren't allowed to pass.

Setting boundaries is one of the best things you can do to ensure the safety of the younger members of your group. Set them as soon as you get to camp and strictly enforce them during the entire trip.

Beware the Silent Killer

There's a silent killer that could come creeping through your campsite and put you to sleep, never to be heard from again. It can't be seen and has no smell, but it's there nonetheless.

That silent killer is carbon monoxide.

The good news is with a little care you can avoid this silent killer because you're the one who creates it. Items like generators, charcoal grills, camp stoves and fuel-powered lanterns all generate carbon monoxide as they operate. Under normal conditions, the carbon monoxide they generate dissipates into the atmosphere and doesn't cause us harm.

Bring one of these devices into an enclosed area where the carbon monoxide doesn't dissipate and you've got a completely different story. In an enclosed area like a tent or a vehicle, carbon monoxide can build up to dangerous levels. Inhale too much of this toxic gas and you could find yourself in deep trouble. Mild carbon monoxide poisoning could result in dizziness, vertigo, confusion, and nausea. If you're exposed for a long period of time, your heart could slow down and eventually stop beating or your central nervous system could be severely impacted to the point that the body stops functioning.

To avoid carbon monoxide, use items that produce it only in well-ventilated areas and keep them out of enclosed areas like your tent. Fall asleep with a gas-powered lantern burning in your tent and you could wake up extremely ill—if you wake up at all.

While most experienced campers know not to use these items in tents, stories abound of inexperienced campers who have perished because of carbon monoxide poisoning. A little common sense goes a long way. If an item burns or has exhaust coming from it, it's more than likely a source of carbon monoxide. Keep it outdoors and don't breathe in the exhaust.

Another source of carbon monoxide poisoning is boats and personal watercraft. People sometimes like to hang out on a rear platform of a boat that's in motion. This may be fun, but it's dangerous because whenever the boat stops or slows down, you're right next to the exhaust. A running boat can quickly fill up with carbon monoxide when the boat is idle and the wind is blowing in the wrong direction. Keep this in mind when out and about on the water.

If you suspect carbon monoxide poisoning has occurred, move the affected person into fresh air and seek immediate medical attention.

It's OK to Have Some Fun

Go into a camping trip planning on being miserable the whole time and guess what? You're probably going to fulfill your prophecy. Go into the same camping trip with an open mind and you might find yourself actually having fun.

Yes, camping is dirty.

Yes, it can be very hot or very cold from time to time.

Yes, there are, YIKES, wild animals out and about.

Yes, there can be insects. Sometimes there are a lot of them.

No, you might not have electricity or running water.

And you know what? That doesn't stop *millions* of people spanning the entire globe from going camping and having a blast. If you think all there is to do while camping is sit in a hot, dusty campsite waiting for the trip to end, you've been going about camping all wrong. Camping trips should be fun for the entire family. The only thing required of you is that you're willing to try something new and go about it with an open mind.

For me, one of the biggest benefits of family camping trips is I get to get away with my family.

During the day, it's all about making sure the kids have a blast, and I have fun watching them have fun exploring nature and enjoying the many things the outdoors have to offer. Once the kids are down for the night, I get to spend quality time with my husband and any other adult family members or friends who came along on the trip. I also manage to squeeze a bit of alone time in, which I spend working on crossword puzzles, catching up on magazines I haven't had time to read at home or perusing a good book.

The rest of this chapter discusses just some of the things people do for fun while camping. Keep in mind that there are a lot of other things you can do, many of which are unique to the particular area where you're camping. Some campgrounds have full rec areas complete with miniature golf and pool tables. I've even stayed places that have full gyms, but working out is the last thing I want to do while I'm camping. I'm there to relax and distress, not to get my heart rate up, but that's just me.

Live a little and relax. It's OK to let yourself have fun while camping.

Go Hiking

Most campgrounds are close multiple trails that lead to scenic points and interesting vistas. When you get bored sitting around in your campsite, you can pass the time by exploring these trails either with your family in tow or without. You can often find everything from easy strolls around lakes and down rivers to grueling treks through dangerous mountain cutbacks within driving distance of a campsite—and sometimes they're part of the park you're camping in.

Hiking and exploring gives you the opportunity to get away from the paved roads and conveniences of society and allows you to experience nature much as our ancestors were able to experience it, with no white noise in the background and no throngs of tourists oohing and aahing. There's nothing more relaxing than hiking alone along a babbling brook in the mountains until you're deep into the woods and then stopping and enjoying the sounds of nature uninterrupted by the sound of passing vehicles and other people.

State parks, regional parks and national parks all usually have hiking trails, many of which lead you to solitary and beautiful areas rife with breathtaking scenery. If you're looking for some of the best sights known to man, you're going to have to be willing to hike in to many of them. The further you get from the pavement, the more likely you are to experience wildlife and nature as Mother Nature created it.

Deer, elk, mountain goats, bison, wolves, you name it. Depending on where you're hiking at, you might have a chance at lucking out and spotting one of these beautiful creatures.

My son and I went for a hike on a trail in Nevada recently and were walking along chatting it up when we came across a group of bighorn sheep. There were 5 of them in the group and when they saw us they slowly moved up the rocky outcropping they'd been grazing on. Three of the bighorn sheep had giant curved horns on their heads and they were a majestic site to see. We definitely wouldn't have seen them if we'd stayed put at the campground because they were extremely skittish around humans, but walking a couple miles up a nearby trail allowed us to get far enough away from camp to where we ran into them. We got some great pictures and now have a story to tell about the time we stumbled across the bighorn sheep.

Hiking is an enjoyable activity, but there are a few things you need to be aware of before you strike off into the wilderness.

Not all trails are created equal and some are created with the extreme hiker or backpacker in mind. Some trails through rough country amount to little more than a tiny path traversing dangerous cliffs and narrow switchbacks. While they can offer a good time for adventurous adults, you wouldn't want to bring your children anywhere near these trails. You also aren't going to want to strike off down one of these trails if you aren't in the best shape of your life—that is, unless you feel like getting airlifted off the mountain when you invariably find yourself in trouble.

It's a good idea to check trails out in advance by scouting them online, so you know whether they're family friendly. If you plan on having young children in tow, look for wide trails in relatively flat areas. The best trails for hiking with young children are typically found near waterways and lakes. If you still have questions or aren't able to find any kid-friendly trails in the area you're planning on staying, call a nearby ranger station. They're usually more than happy to point you in the right direction.

Create a plan detailing the path you plan on taking and map it out in advance. Setting off into the wilderness on an unknown course is a recipe for disaster. Trails can crisscross one another and there may be multiple forks in the trail along the way. Plan your route ahead of time and stick to it. Leave your plan with someone who isn't going hiking with you and let them know when you plan on being back, so if you don't return on time they'll know exactly where to start the search.

When creating a hiking plan, it helps to keep in mind the average person can hike 2 to 3 miles an hour under optimal conditions on flat land. If you have older people, people that are out of shape or children in the hiking party, it can be much less than that. It can also be much less than that if you're like me and want to stop and smell every flower along the way. If the trails are steep or are at a high altitude, that'll slow you down, too.

The longest trip most people are going to want to do in a single day is a 5 to 10 mile round trip and that's only if there are no young children along. Start your trips early in the day and you'll be able to enjoy the hike more than if you start in the afternoon and have to rush to get done before dark.

Keep in mind that it's the slowest member of your party that dictates the pace and plan accordingly. It doesn't matter how good of shape you're in if you have someone in tow who isn't in as good of shape. You're going to end up stopping and waiting on them, so plan your trip based on the shape the weakest member of your party is in.

Print out a map of the area you're hiking in and carry it and an ink pen or pencil with you. Each time you come to a fork in the trail, you can write it on your map, along with an identifying landmark or two. When it's time to head back to civilization, all you have to do is flip the map over and follow your trail back. Keep in mind that the way back is going to look different than the way there. Many a hiker has thought they were on the wrong trail because the way back looked so different they felt it couldn't possibly be the same path. Stop periodically and turn around and look at the way things are going to look on the way back. Identify landmarks you can use to make sure you're headed in the right direction and write them down.

Don't think for a second you can rely on GPS to get you home. Signals are notoriously spotty in remote areas and just because your GPS works at the trailhead, there's no guarantee it'll work once you're a mile or two in. Maps don't lose their signal, so always carry a paper map with you.

No matter what you do, always stay on the trail.

While it may be tempting to head off on your own to explore interesting photo ops and uncharted territory, this is also a great way to become hopelessly lost. If you do find yourself lost, don't attempt to find your way back to the trail. The whistle and flashlight you packed (you did pack a whistle and flashlight, right?) can be used to signal rescuers when you don't make it back to camp on time.

If you're a bit out of shape (or a lot, as I was before I started hiking regularly), the higher altitude trails are going to do a number on you. I remember my first camping trip to the mountains. I thought I was in pretty good shape because I'd been working out for a couple months preparing myself to hike to the top of Yosemite Falls in Yosemite National Park in California. The hike is a 7-mile round trip and I thought I was in pretty good shape because I'd hiked a 10-mile loop around a reservoir near my house a week earlier. Boy was I wrong. The elevation and the uphill stretches got to me and I was winded within the first mile. I had to stop every thirty seconds and rest in order to avoid passing out and tumbling off the side of the cliff. After the second mile, I started to sound like I was in an old war movie. I vaguely remember grabbing my husband and dramatically shouting something to the effect of, "I'm not going to make it. Just go on without me. I'll be here when you get back." He didn't leave my side, bless his soul, and I finally made it to the top of the falls. The view was breathtaking.

I begged my husband to call in a rescue chopper, but he refused. We finally made it back down the trail, a full 12 hours from the time we started.

Just because you're able to do something at a lower altitude doesn't mean you're going to be able to do the same thing at a higher altitude in the same amount of time. If you go hiking on trails in the mountains, be prepared to rest a lot and bring along plenty of water and food. That's actually good advice no matter where you're hiking. You never know how long you're going to be out and you don't want to get stranded somewhere with no food and water. While that mountain stream you've been following may look refreshing, you never know what it could be contaminated with. If you end up having to drink water of unknown quality from a natural source, you could get extremely sick. Harmful microorganisms are invisible to the naked eye and just because water looks clean doesn't mean it is.

There are a several items you should always carry with you when you're hiking:

A day pack to carry everything in. Invest in a lightweight and comfortable day pack with padded shoulder straps. If you're only planning on going on short hikes, a small day pack will suffice. If you're planning on doing longer hikes, an internal or external frame pack can help distribute the load of all of the stuff you're going to want to carry.

A compass. If you get lost, a compass can help you orient yourself. Make sure you learn how to use your compass before you need it.

A flashlight and extra batteries. Always carry a flashlight and extra batteries with you. If you get lost, the flashlight can be used to signal a rescue party.

Fire starter. You won't need this if everything goes according to plan. If not, you're going to be glad you have it. A lighter will usually suffice. You can pack a flint and striker if you know how to use one.

A map of the area and a pen or pencil. A trail map is one of the most important items to take with you when hiking. You can mark off the path you're taking and any forks in the road. You can also indicate landmarks you can use on the way back to help ensure you find your way.

A multitool. A multitool like a Leatherman can come in handy on the trail. It can be used to repair damaged gear and is great to have if you get lost.

A small first aid kit. Keep a small first aid kit in your bag that has antiseptic wipes, bandages, pain killers, sterile pads, tape and scissors in it, at a bare minimum. Be sure to pack any special medications you think you might need.

A whistle. This is another item that's good to have on hand in an emergency situation. Carry a loud whistle and you'll up your odds of being found quickly if you become lost.

Biodegradable toilet paper. This one's self-explanatory. Outhouses are few and far between on the trail and sometimes nature's call has to be answered, especially after a night of cocktails, s'mores and barbecue food. You don't want to have to wipe with leaves . . . trust me on this one.

Food (or at least snacks, if the hike will be a short one). Lightweight snacks that are high in calories like protein bars and trail mix are great for hiking food. Pack more than you think you're going to need. Hiking burns a lot of calories and you're going to be hungry. You don't want to get halfway through your hike and run out of snacks.

Plenty of water. Again, pack more than you think you're going to need. You're going to be thirsty. Really thirsty. Running out of water can really ruin a good time.

Sunscreen. Apply sunscreen liberally and then reapply it as needed. That is, unless you want to end up looking like a walking piece of beef jerky by the time you reach your golden years.

A jacket or heavy sweatshirt. Even if you plan on getting back long before the sun goes down, pack a jacket or heavy sweatshirt for each person in your group. The weather can change in an instant and you'll be glad you did if something happens and you end up out on the trail when the sun goes down.

A camera. You never know what you're going to come across on a hike. You're going to want to be able to take pictures.

A watch. It's all too easy to lose track of time on the trail. Carry a watch with you so you'll know when it's time to turn around and head back.

Wear comfortable clothing and invest in a nice pair of light trail shoes or hiking boots—and be sure to break them in before setting off on a long hike. New shoes can be extremely uncomfortable until they're broken in and blisters are all-too-common on the trail. Broken-in shoes that fit well and good socks can go a long way toward alleviating blisters (and foot pain in general).

Start off slow and pick hikes that are within your limitations. Attempting to hike to the top of Half Dome on your first hiking trip is asking for disappointment—and maybe quite a bit of pain and suffering. For those who don't know, Half Dome is a strenuous 14+ mile hike to the top of a large rock in Yosemite Park in California. At the end of the hike, you have to traverse up the infamous cable section, using cables to climb your way up the steep rock face to the top of the Dome. If you're going to attempt a hike like this on your first attempt at hiking, take out a good life insurance policy ahead of time.

Hiking and exploring trails is a great way to have fun, as long as you hike safely and don't try to do too much. Know your limitations and plan hiking trips everyone in your group will be able to enjoy.

Just to review, here are the safety rules you should follow before and during a hiking trip:

Before the Trip

Make sure you're physically fit enough to handle the hiking trip you're planning.

Plan your route.

Print out or purchase a trail map of the area.

Let a friend or family member know where you're going and when you plan on returning.

Pack the gear mentioned earlier in this chapter. Make sure it's all in good working order.

During the Trip

Watch your step.

Stay on the trail.

Be prepared for inclement weather.

Don't try to cross a stream that's flowing too fast to safely traverse. Some trails will be blocked by fast-running water in the spring or during unexpected storms.

Keep a close eye on the kids. Don't hike trails that are beyond their skill level. You don't want to end up carrying an exhausted child while walking a trail.

Don't deviate from your chosen path.

Always check footholds and handholds before placing your weight on them. If you slip, you could end up taking everyone below you out as you go.

Don't overestimate your abilities.

Stop and look behind you periodically. You'll be surprised how different things look going in the opposite direction.

What to Do If You're Lost

It's unlikely to happen if you're careful and stick to the planned route, but there's a slight chance you could find yourself off the trail and unable to find it—or on an unfamiliar trail that leads into the unknown. Make sure you and everyone in your party is well-versed on what to do if they get lost, especially any children you have with you. Every person in your party should have their own food, water, whistle and flashlight. That way, if they get separated from the group, they'll be able to alert the rest of the party immediately. If they're separated for any period of time, having their own water and food could save their life.

Here's what you need to do if you get lost:

- **As soon as the lost person realizes they're separated from the group, the person should stop and stay in place.** Continuing to walk could move them further in the wrong direction. The closer they are to the trail, the faster they'll be found.
- **Start blowing the whistle immediately.** Chances are the rest of the group will still be close enough to hear you. If you're hiking alone, blow the whistle once every few minutes and

listen for a response. If you hear a response, continue blowing the whistle until you're found.

- **Adults in the group can pick a landmark in the area where they're lost and can walk a distance from the landmark, keeping it in sight while looking for the trail.** They can then walk back to the landmark and try again in a different direction. Having a compass on-hand and knowing how to use it can help you head in the right direction. If you aren't sure, you're probably better off waiting where you are, unless you're in danger of starving or dying of dehydration.
- **Don't rush.** If you panic and rush off, you're more likely to find yourself hopelessly lost.
- **Stay close to an open area.** If you're lost and are hunkered down in a thick stand of trees, you're a lot less likely to be found than you are if you're in an open area. If you don't want to be exposed to the elements, use rocks to create an S.O.S. message and an arrow pointing to where you're at.
- **A fire can be used to create a smoke signal by day and a flame to guide rescuers at night.** Make sure you clear a wide enough area around your fire to where you won't start a forest fire. That's the last thing you need when lost in the wilderness.

It helps to keep in mind the vast majority of hikers never find themselves in trouble. Carrying safety gear that you know how to use and keeping trail safety in mind will ensure you aren't part of the unfortunate minority. Many of the hikers who find themselves in big trouble end up that way because they don't know how to safely hike and follow trails.

A little education goes a long way.

Hit the Water

Rare is the campsite that doesn't have some type of water nearby. Rivers, lakes, ponds and swimming pools all offer unique activities you can partake in to stave off boredom. There are literally thousands of things you can do in, around and on bodies of water.

The following are some of the more common water-related activities:

Boating

If you have a boat, you're probably no stranger to the long list of activities a boat opens up to you. You can find a quiet cove away from the crowded areas those without boats frequent where you can hang out and swim, fish or just relax for as long as you'd like.

You can explore the body of water you're on, looking for something that piques your interest. You can also go skiing, tubing or wakeboarding, which are more strenuous, but are good ways to keep older kids and teenagers entertained.

No boat? No problem—many of the larger lakes and waterways have places you can rent a boat from.

Diving and Snorkeling

Tired of being above the water? Get below it by taking a diving or snorkeling trip. In a clear body of water, you'll be amazed by the vegetation and sea life there is swimming below the surface.

Fishing

If you're near a body of water that's been around for a while and is at least a few feet deep, there's a pretty good chance there's fish in it.

New bodies of water can be tough to fish.

Bring your children with you to a local tackle shop and ask for help. Locals are much more likely to divulge information to a woman with children in tow, so ladies, this one's up to you. You never know . . . the tips you get may help the kids catch dinner.

Be sure to check with your local fish and game agency to see if there are heavy metals or other contaminants in the water. You don't want to eat the fish if there are.

Float around

Procure something that floats. Anything big enough to hold you afloat will work. A raft, a life vest, an inner tube, etc. Hop in the water and float around for a while. Be careful you don't float too far out to sea or you're going to have a tough time getting back.

If you do find yourself stranded, as I'm embarrassed to admit I once did when I fell asleep, flag down a passing boat. They'll get a kick out of your story and should be willing to return you to shore.

Rafting

If there's a river with a decent current nearby, floating down it in a raft can be a ton of fun. Some rivers are slow enough to enjoy in an inner tube, while others require large rafts and aren't for the faint of heart.

Skipping rocks

Want a quick detour to the water to distract bored kids?
Find a body of water—pretty much any body of water will do—and teach your kids to skip rocks. Flat rocks work best. Throw the rock so it hits the water and the flat side skims across the water. Skilled stone skippers can get a rock to skip 20 or more times before it sinks below the surface. How many times can you get a rock to skip? We keep records for the day, the trip and there's an all-time record of 10 skips set by my husband that no one else in the family has yet come close to.

Swimming

Find a lake, pond or swimming pool and hop in. Kids love to spend hours swimming. Be sure to slather on copious amounts of sunscreen and don't forget to reapply regularly. You don't want to cope with nasty sunburns later on when you get back to camp. Find a place where other children are swimming and your kids will have even more fun.

Sports and Recreational Games

Get off your butt and get active.

There are all sorts of sports and recreational games you can engage in while camping. It's as easy as bringing a ball or some gear and finding a good spot. Here are a handful of ideas to get you started:

Baseball

As long as you have room to pack the gear, baseball (or softball, for that matter) can be a fun way to pass time. Don't have room for all the gear? A broomstick and a couple tennis balls can be just as much fun.

Bike riding

You can buy a bike rack that allows you to attach bicycles to the back of your vehicle or you can call ahead and find a place that rents bicycles by the day. Some campsites have bikes available for a nominal fee.

Capture the flag

While your kids may have played the video game version of capture the flag in popular video games like Halo and Call of Duty, they probably haven't played the real-life game it's based on.

Two groups of kids are split up into teams, each of which has a flag. The goal of the game is to sneak into the opposing team's base and grab their flag without getting tagged out. When a player gets tagged on the opposing team's side, the player has to return to their base for a designated amount of time before heading out again. The winner is the first team to capture the opposing team's flag and return it to their base without getting caught.

Corn hole

Also called bean bag toss and baggo, to play corn hole all you need are 8 bean bags and 2 flat surfaces that are 2 feet by 4 feet with a 6" hole centered 9 inches down from the top of the platforms. The back end of the platforms should be raised a foot off the ground, leaving the platform sitting at an angle. Separate the platforms so there is 27 feet between the bottom edges of the platform.

Here are the rules of the game:

- Play is divided into innings, in which each player throws 4 bean bags.
- Players must stand behind the bottom edge of one of the platforms and throw at the other platform. Crossing in front of the bottom edge is a foul and no points are scored for the toss. Players can stand on one side of the platform or the other, but all throws by a player in a single inning must be from the same side.
- Bags thrown through the hole are worth 3 points.
- Bags that land on and stay on the board until the end of the inning are worth 1 point. Bags that touch the ground first and bounce onto the board aren't scored.
- If a player from one team lands a bag in the hole and it's followed up by a hole shot from the other

player, the shots cancel each other out and no points are scored.

- The game is won by the first player or team to reach 21 points.

Disc golf

I don't know whether this holds true nationwide, but a number of campgrounds and parks in my area have disc golf courses set up that can be used for free or for a nominal fee.

The game is played similar to golf, but you use a Frisbee instead of a club and balls. The goal is to get the Frisbee into the basket in as few throws as possible.

Don't have a course near you? Not a problem. An empty garbage can makes a great basket and can be moved around to create different "holes" to play.

Football

Whether playing a full-on flag football game, two-hand touch or just tossing a ball around, football can be a great way to pass time while camping.

Hide and Seek

Here's an oldie, but goody.

Hide and seek is a time-honored game that kids nowadays rarely play. A base is chosen at the start of the game. One person is it and counts to a predetermined number while the rest of the players hide. When the person who is it finished counting, he or she sets off looking for the hidden players. Players try to make it back to a designated base before they're caught by the it person. The last person caught gets to choose who is it for the next game.

Horseshoes

Tossing horseshoes at a peg may not sound like fun, but it's actually a great way to pass the time.

Here's a quick and easy rundown of the rules to get you started:

- Games are either played until someone reaches 40 points or there are 40 shoes thrown by each person. Your call.
- Each player gets two horseshoes to pitch. One player pitches his horseshoes, and they're followed by the next player's horseshoes.
- Shoes have to be within a horseshoe's width of the stake to be scored.
- The closest horseshoe to the stake scores one point in each round. If both of your shoes are closer than your opponent's, you get 2 points.
- Ringers occur when the horseshoe encircles the stake. If you place a straight edge across the gap in the horseshoe and it touches the stake, it doesn't count as a ringer. Ringers are worth 3 points. A ringer is cancelled if another player throws a ringer on top of it.
- If you have a ringer and the closest horseshoe in a round, you get 4 points.
- Leaners are shoes that are leaning against the stake. They count as one point. Ringers are

considered closer to the stake than leaners when considering who gets the points for the closest stake.

Ladder toss

This game is played by throwing *bolas*, which are 2 balls connected by strings, at a PVC pipe ladder that has 3 rungs. The top ladder is worth 1 point, the middle ladder 2 and the bottom ladder 3. Having a bola on each rung is worth 10 points. Most games are played to 21 points and some variations of the game reverse the scoring, so the top rung is worth 3.

Lawn bowling

In this game, players roll 4 bowls in an attempt to get them the closest to a smaller white ball, known as a jack. Points are scored for each bowl the player has that's closer to the jack than the other player's bowls.

Rock climbing

Inexperienced climbers should take lessons before attempting to climb on their own. Rock climbing is a fun, albeit rather demanding, way to kill time. It isn't for the faint of heart, but those in good shape with an adventurous side will love this pastime.

Soccer

Grab a soccer ball and set up a couple cones as goals and you've got a makeshift soccer goal that can be used for pickup games and shooting practice.

Spelunking

Hire a guide and go exploring local caves. You'll be amazed by some of the stuff you find underground. Stalactites, stalagmites and all sorts of other interesting rock formations can be found deep beneath the surface of the earth.

Tag

Tag is a playground games that can be played while camping. It involves one player or a team of players chasing other players in an attempt to tag them. When an opposing player is tagged, they either become "it" or are out of the game until the next round.

There are a number of variations on the game of tag. Here are some of the more popular versions of tag:

- **Ball tag.** The "it" person uses a ball to tag opposing players, either by rolling it at them or throwing it at them. Make sure you use soft balls for this game.
- **British Bulldog.** This game is played in a rectangular play area. Two players start in the middle and all the other players start at one end of the play area. The goal is for the players to run to the other end without being tagged by the players in the middle.
- **Chain tag.** When a player is tagged they have to hold hands with the "it" player, creating a chain of players that has to work together to run other players down. The players at the end of the chain

are the only ones who can tag someone out because they're the only ones with a free hand.

- **Elimination tag.** The tagged players are out of the game. The game ends when the "it" person has tagged everyone out. The last person to be tagged out in the game chooses the "it" person for the next round.
- **Flashlight tag.** This game is played at night and players attempt to tag other players using the beams of light emitted from a flashlight.
- **Freeze tag.** Tagged players are frozen in place and must stay where they are until they're tagged by a player who isn't it.
- **Bomb's away.** The "it" player throws a soft ball as high as he or she can in the air. As soon as the ball is thrown, all players take off away from the "it" person. When he or she catches the ball and shouts "Bomb's away!" all of the other players have to stop. The "it" player is then allowed to take 2 large steps toward any player they'd like. If they then throw the ball and hit the player, that player is out of the game. They can then start from where that player is and take two more steps toward any other player on the field. If they throw the ball and hit that player, that player is out. The game continues until the "it" person has hit all of the players in the game or has missed with three throws.
- **Shadow tag.** Players try to step on the shadow of other players to tag them out. In my experience, this game results in a lot of arguing about

whether or not a person's shadow was indeed stepped on.

- **Zombie tag.** One person starts off as a zombie and everyone else is human. As the zombie tags other players, they become zombies as well. The game continues until one person is left. That person wins the game and starts the next game as the zombie.
- **Wood tag.** Players are considered safe and can't be tagged out when touching something made of wood.

Washers

The rules vary depending on where in the nation you're playing washers, but the basic premise is the same. Toss washers into a cup to score points.

1" washers are the washers of choice and the cups are set into a platform or dug into the ground so they're level with the surface around them. Paint them different colors in groups of 4, so you'll be able to tell them apart during a game.

Here's a general scoring system you can use to play the game of washers:

- Washers that land in the cup are worth 5 points. If a player throws a washer in the cup after an opposing player lands a washer in it, the score is cancelled out and neither player scores.
- A hanger is a washer that hangs over the edge of the cup, but doesn't fall in. These are worth 2

points if the hole in the washer doesn't extend over the edge of the cup and 3 if it does.

- If no one gets a washer in the cup or a hanger, the player with the washer closest to the cup is awarded one point.
- The winner is the first person or team to reach or pass 21 points.

Card Games

Not into activities that are physically exerting? Don't worry; you don't have to sit around bored. Card games are a great way to pass time without ever having to leave the campsite. They're a fun way to wrap up a long day and wind down before bed.

Get out a deck of cards and gather around the campfire. These games are fun for the whole family and easy enough that all but the smallest members of the family should be able to join in.

Go Fish

Players: 3 to 6
Supplies needed: 1 deck of cards

Rules:

Shuffle the deck and deal 5 cards to each player. Place the remaining cards face down in a draw pile. The goal of the game is to collect sets of 4 cards that are the same rank.

The first player picks one of the other players and asks for a card. The player asking for the card has to have at least one of the cards they're asking for in their deck. If the player has the card being requested, they have to give it to the requestor. The requestor then gets to continue his or her turn and can ask the same player or another player for a card.

If the player doesn't have the card being requested, the player says "go fish" and the requestor has to draw the top card from the draw pile. If it's the card the player requested, the player shows it to the group and gets to continue his or her turn. If not, the player's turn is over and play is passed to the person to the left of the player.

When a set of four cards of the same rank is collected, the player holding the cards reveals the cards to the group and then places them face down in a pile in front of themselves.

Play continues until the draw pile runs out or one of the players has no cards left in their hand. The player with the most sets of cards at this time is declared the winner.

Liar

Players: At least 3
Supplies needed: 1 to 2 decks of cards

Rules:

Shuffle the deck of cards and deal the cards until all cards have been dealt. The goal of the game is to be the first player to get rid of all of the cards being held.

To get rid of cards, you place a number of cards of the same type face down in the middle of the table and announce what they are. For example, you could place 4 jacks in the middle and announce "4 jacks." You're allowed to lie about what you're placing on the table. You could place 2 jacks and 2 queens face down on the table and announce "4 jacks."

Once the cards are placed on the table, the other players have the opportunity to accuse the player of lying by announcing "Liar." If no one accuses the player of lying, the cards are left face down and put in the discard pile. If someone announces "Liar," the cards are flipped over to check and see if the player is lying or not. If the player is caught lying, the "Liar" must take all of the cards in the discard pile. If the person told the truth about what was being discarded, the accuser must take all of the cards in the discard pile.

The game continues until all of the players except one have gotten rid of their cards. The winner is the first person to get rid of his or her cards.

Old Maid

Players: 3 to 8
Supplies needed: A deck of cards, with three of the queens removed from the deck.

Rules:

The one queen left in the deck is the Old Maid. The goal is to be one of the players that aren't holding the Old Maid at the end of the game.

A designated dealer should shuffle the deck and deal the cards evenly to the group. If some players have more cards than others, it's OK. Once all of the cards have been dealt, players look at their cards and place any pairs they find face down in front of them.

The dealer allows the player to his left to draw one card. If a matching pair is made, the player discards the pair. If not, the player adds the card to his or her hand and keeps it. This player then allows the player to his or her left to draw a card and do the same.

Play continues around the circle until the only card left is the Old Maid. The player holding the Old Maid at the end of the game loses the game.

Slap Jack

Players: 2 to 5
Supplies needed: 1 deck of cards

Rules:

Deal all of the cards to the players. It doesn't matter if players have uneven numbers of cards. The cards are placed face-down in a pile in front of each player.

The player to the left of the dealer flips the top card on his pile over and places it in the center of the play area. If it's any card other than a Jack, play continues on to the next player. If the card is a Jack, the first person to slap their hand over the Jack is the winner of the pile of cards in the middle.

Once a player loses all of his or her cards, that player is out of the game. That is, unless he's able to slap the next Jack that's laid down. Out players can only slap the next Jack laid down after they run out of cards. After that, they're permanently out. The last person left in the game is declared the winner.

Spoons

Players: 3 to 7
Supplies needed: 3 decks of cards and spoons. The number of spoons will be equal to the total number of players

minus one. For example, a game with 5 players would use 4 spoons.

Rules:

Play this game by circling your chairs around a central location to which each player has equal access. Place the spoons in the middle of the play area. The handles of the spoons should be facing outward.

Four cards should be dealt to each player. The player is allowed to pick these cards up and look at them. The rest of the cards are dealt face-down to each player. Each player goes in a circle and draws a card from their pile and adds it to their hand. If a player gets 4 of a kind, the player reaches out and grabs a spoon. As soon as the other players see the player reach for a spoon, they can all try to grab a spoon as well. The player left without a spoon is out of the game.

Remove one spoon from the play area and continue the game until all but one player has been eliminated.

A variant of this game has the dealer deal 4 cards to each player and then place the deck next to him. He then draws the top card from the deck and either keeps it or discards it by placing it in front of the player to the left of him. If he discards a card, he must draw another card from the top of the deck and keep it. If the dealer keeps the first card, he must draw the top card and place it in front of the player next to him without looking at it.

Play continues to the player the dealer passed the card to. The player checks the card in front of him and either passes it and draws a new card or keeps the card and places a new card in front of the player to his left. This continues around the circle until someone gets 4 of a kind and reaches for a spoon. Everyone tries to grab a spoon and the person without a spoon is eliminated, their cards are added to the bottom of the deck and play continues around the circle until all but one player has been eliminated.

UNO

Uno is a fun game that requires a special deck of UNO cards to play. The rules can get a bit complicated, but each deck of UNO cards comes complete with the rules. Up to 10 players are able to play at once using a single deck. Because of the number of players that can play, this is a good game for large groups of people.

War

Players: 2
Supplies needed: 1 deck of cards.

Rules:

Shuffle the deck and deal the cards evenly between the two players. Each player should place the cards face down in front of them without looking at them.

The players take the top card off of the deck and flip it over. The player holding the card with the highest face value wins the round and gets to keep both cards. Here's the face value order of the cards, from highest to lowest:

- Ace
- King
- Queen

- Jack
- 10
- 9
- 8
- 7
- 6
- 5
- 4
- 3
- 2

If two cards with the same face value are played, War is declared. Each player states "I declare War" while laying down a card with each syllable of the statement. The 4th card is placed faced up and the winner is the player with the card with the highest face value. If the face value is a tie again, another War is declared. The winner of any War wins all of the cards in the pile.

The player to take the entire deck of cards is the winner. Alternatively, the person with the most cards after a set frame of time or a certain number of Wars is declared the winner.

Cooking While Camping

I don't know whether it's because the days are spent running around and having fun and you return to camp tired and hungry, but there's nothing as good as eating a well-cooked dinner by the light of a campfire. Camp food tastes great, is filling and cooking and eating around the campfire is a good way to wrap up a great day.

Cooking food over a campfire allows you to experience mealtime much in the same manner the pioneers experienced it when first exploring the nation. Some campers bring along a barbecue and a camp stove as well. I use a camp stove from time to time, but the barbecue is left at home. Any grilling or barbecuing is done on a grate placed over the campfire.

The downside to cooking in camp is it's much slower than cooking at home. You have to be patient and willing to improvise when it comes to cooking techniques and food preparation. Set aside plenty of time for cooking meals because you're going to need it.

There are a number of methods you can use to cook while camping. The following methods are some of the more common methods.

Camp Stoves

Bring along a camp stove and you'll be able to cook in a manner similar to the way you'd cook on a gas stove at home. A double-burner camp stove will give you two burners you can use at the same time to speed up the cooking process.

Push-button ignition stoves are the easiest because all you have to do is press a button and the stove lights itself. At least they work that way the first few times you light them. Once they age a bit, they tend to require multiple pushes of the button until the stars align correctly and the stove finally lights. My husband typically ends up using a lighter or matches to light our fancy push button stoves because it's easier and less frustrating.

Lightweight stoves are available that are geared toward backpackers, but this isn't a necessity for the weekend camper. If you plan on backpacking, a small single-burner stove is a good option.

Liquid gas stoves burn fuels like kerosene or white gas. They have refillable gas tanks designed to hold a number of different fuel types. The tanks are usually detachable, so you only have to take the tank in to get it filled. These stoves are bulky and heavy, but they burn hotter and have adjustable flames that can be used in most weather conditions.

Cartridge stoves are less expensive and lighter than liquid gas stoves, but they aren't as durable as their bulkier counterparts. They use gas cartridges filled with gases like propane or butane. The cartridges are one-time use items that are thrown away once they're empty. These stoves burn clean and are easier to use than liquid gas stoves, except for when the wind picks up or the weather cools down to below 35 degrees F, at which time they're tough to keep lit. You can purchase a heat exchanger that'll allow you to use your stove in cooler temperatures.

Cartridge stoves are a good choice if you're concerned with weight because the cartridges are light and some cartridges can be used to light both lanterns and cartridge stoves. If weight and space isn't of concern, you're better off going with a liquid gas stove.

Camp stoves are rated by their *efficiency*, which is the amount of time it takes for the stove to completely deplete a full fuel canister or tank when turned all the way up, and *boil time*, which is the amount of time it takes for the stove to bring one quart of water to a boil at sea level when the air temperature is 70 degrees F and the stove is turned all the way up. The efficiency of the stove isn't much of a concern as long as you bring along enough fuel to last you the entire trip. The boil time indicates how hot the stove burns. Lower boil times mean it's going to take a longer time to cook your food.

You could spend a lot of money on the latest and greatest technology in camp stoves, but that really isn't necessary. Walk around any campground and you're likely to find most campers have a 2-burner propane camp stove, usually made by Coleman. Save yourself some cash and buy a Coleman camp stove, which won't break the bank and is the brand of choice for many happy campers across the nation. They cost less than a hundred bucks and will make short work of breakfast, coffee and pretty much any other cooking task you'd want to engage in while camping.

There's no real need to get too fancy with your cook stove. As long as you have a flame and stable place to set your stove, you should be good to go.

Charcoal Barbecues

You can bring a charcoal barbecue along with you or you can bring a grate and use a fire ring with charcoal. If you've barbecued at home with charcoal, you already know how to use a charcoal barbecue. You can get a similar effect by lighting a wood fire and letting the wood burn down until there are nothing but hot coals left.

Here's a quick primer on getting charcoal started:

1. Clear the grill of ash and dirt before starting it.
2. Remove the grate from the grill.
3. If there are vents on the bottom of the grill, set them to the open position.
4. Arrange the briquettes in a pyramid at the bottom of the grill.
5. Add lighter fluid to the briquettes and let it soak in.
6. Light the briquettes using a long lighter or a match. Don't stand too close to the grill because it can light up quickly if you used a lot of lighter fluid.
7. If the grill is dirty from being previously used, put the grill back on while the flame is burning and let the heat burn the grease and grime off of the grill. Scrape it with a wire brush once the flames go down.
8. Let the charcoal burn until the coals are covered with a light coating of thin ash and are glowing red.

9. Spread the charcoal out and place any half-lit pieces between coals that are completely lit and burning red. Don't add more lighter fluid. This will make the food taste like lighter fluid and may put out the lit charcoals.
10. You're ready to cook. Get to it.

Briquettes are available that claim not to need lighter fluid, but I've found they're hit and miss. The brand name self-igniting briquettes work well, but the cheaper brands won't stay lit. It's up to you whether you want to pay extra for the self-lighting briquettes.

The Charcoal Chimney

A *charcoal chimney* can be used to ensure briquettes light without use of lighter fluid.

The typical charcoal chimney is a metal cylinder into which briquettes are place. The briquettes at the bottom of the chimney are lit using newspaper or starter cubes and the coals burn evenly from the bottom up. The chimney helps the coals light up faster and they'll be ready to cook on in a shorter amount of time. When the coals are ready, dump them into the barbecue or fire pit you're ready to cook.

Here's a pro tip to help you get your coals started right. When you add newspaper to the bottom, crumple it lightly and add a bit of cooking oil to the newspaper. More air equals more oxygen for the fire and the cooking oil will help get the newspaper lit and keep it burning long enough to light up your coals.

Charcoal Grilling Tips

The following tips should help you successfully grill food on a charcoal barbecue:

- **Don't constantly turn your food or you run the risk of drying it out.** Ideally, you want to cook it completely on one side before flipping and cooking the other side.
- **Don't pack your food too tightly onto the grill.** You want to leave air space around your food in order to allow it to cook evenly.
- **Lighter cubes can be used to light charcoal.** Place a lighter cube beneath the charcoal pyramid and light the cube. The charcoal will then light from the bottom up.
- **Sauces with sugar in them will burn easily.** Don't put them on until you're almost done with the meat.
- **Spray non-stick cooking spray on your grill to keep food from sticking to it.**
- **Use a spray bottle with water in it to knock down any flames that rise up because of grease hitting the coals.** Flames are problematic because they char your meat and cause it to cook unevenly.

Direct and Indirect Grilling

Direct grilling is a cooking process in which the meat is placed on the grill directly over the hot coals. It's the method most people use for barbecuing. Direct grilling is the best method of grilling for sausages, individual pieces of chicken, steak, pork chops and ground meat.

Indirect grilling places the food you're cooking on the grill so it isn't placed directly above the coals. The coals are on one side of the grill and the meat is placed on the grate on the other side. Food cooks more slowly with the indirect grilling, which is recommended for larger foods like whole birds, ribs and tough meats like brisket and pork shoulder. It can also be used to grill delicate foods like certain types of fish that would be destroyed by direct heat.

When indirect grilling is used, most meats benefit from a quick five or six minute searing. To sear meat and lock in the flavor, place it over direct heat for 2 to 3 minutes on each side. It'll cook the outside of the meat, leaving the inside soft and tender. Move it to indirect heat to finish the cooking process.

Wood Fire

Cooking over a wood fire is one of my favorite ways to cook up a camp meal. Food can be cooked on a grill over a wood fire or you can use pots and pans to cook up a wide variety of foods. Your campfire can be used to cook breakfast, lunch and dinner as long as you keep it going and periodically add wood to keep it hot.

The best part about using a wood fire is the smoky, woody flavor it imparts to the food. The flavor of your food largely depends on the type of wood used to build the fire. Oak, applewoods, nut woods and a number of other woods can be used, and all impart a unique flavor to the foods that are cooked over them. Avoid woods like pine that impart a bitter taste to food.

The following woods are popular choices for cooking over:

- **Alder.**
- **Apple.**
- **Cedar.**
- **Cherry.**
- **Hickory.**
- **Maple.**
- **Mesquite.**
- **Nut woods.**
- **Oak.**

An adjustable cast-iron grill that sits on legs that rest on both sides of the grill will make life much easier if you plan on cooking over your campfire. Meats can be grilled directly on the grill and pots and pans can be placed onto the grill for foods you don't want to cook over an open flame. Adjustable grills can be moved up and down, so you're able to control how close your food is to the fire.

If you really want to go all out, invest in a *Dutch oven* or a cauldron that can be placed directly into the fire. Make sure you read up on how to properly season a Dutch oven before use. Using one of these allows you to slowly cook up a number of delicious soups and stews. You haven't lived until you've had clam chowder made from clams you just caught at the beach and cooked up in a Dutch oven.

Campfire Cooking Tips

The following tips will help you successfully cook over a campfire:

- **Dry, seasoned woods are best for campfire cooking.** They make hotter burning fires with less smoke, which is what you ideally want to cook over.

- **You don't have to wait for the fire to burn all the way down to cook over a wood fire.** In fact, small flames can be used to sear meat and add extra flavor to it. If flare-ups occur, you can move your meat away from the flare-ups to another area of the grill.

- **Set aside plenty of time for building the campfire and getting it to a point where it's ready to be cooked over.** It can take as long as a couple hours for logs to be reduced to coals that are easy to cook over.

- **You can practice indirect cooking with wood fires.** Let the wood burn down to coals with no flames. Move the coals to one side of the fire pit and place the food you want to indirectly cook on the other side.

The Campfire: An Age-Old Tradition

The campfire is an age-old tradition that has probably been around since man invented fire. It's definitely been around for hundreds, if not thousands or millions, of years. I can picture Grug the caveman sitting around a campfire bragging to other cavemen about the mammoth that got away. Fast forward a million or so years to last few centuries and our forefathers sat around campfires for warmth and used them to cook food and warm coffee much in the same way we do today.

If you've never built a campfire before, the first time you try to build one can be an exercise in frustration, especially if you're trying to build a fire on a windy day. Let's take a look at the steps involved in building a campfire:

1. If you're lucky, the campsite will already have a fire ring or fire pit. If it does, use the already made ring or pit. Skip ahead to step 5. If not, you're going to have to build a fire ring or pit yourself.
2. Clear the area around where you're going to build your campfire ring. You don't want a loose ember to be able to get away and start a fire. Remove all organic material and anything flammable from an area that's at least 10 feet in all directions from the location where you plan on building the fire.
3. You can dig a fire pit if you want. Some camp areas require use of a fire pit. Dig the pit to 6" to 12" deep

and 2 to 4 feet wide. A fire pit will provide an added layer of protection from the wind.

4. Gather dry rocks and use them to build a circle around your fire pit. Wet rocks should not be used, as they can explode when heated. Fit the rocks together as tightly as you can. The rock also provides protection from the wind. Stack the rocks until the ring is at least a foot tall and fill in any gaps with smaller rocks or gravel.
5. Now that you've got your fire ring built, it's time to build your campfire. Gather *tinder*, which consists of small twigs and dry grass and leaves, and *kindling*, which are small sticks. You're also going to need larger pieces of wood to burn in your fire.
6. Pile a couple handfuls of tinder in the center of the fire ring.
7. Crisscross the smaller kindling over the tinder.
8. Light the tinder. It should flare up and start to ignite the kindling.
9. Blow gently on the tinder to help stoke the flame. If necessary, light the tinder in a handful of places.
10. As the kindling catches fire, add more kindling to get a good fire going. Begin adding larger pieces of wood one at a time until you get the fire going.
11. Keep the fire going by adding pieces of wood as necessary. Be careful not to add too much fuel to the fire because you don't want it to get out of control.

Sitting around a campfire at the end of a long day is a great way to wrap the day up. It's easy to get comfortable around the fire, but you do need to keep a few responsibilities in mind while maintaining and enjoying your fire. Children and pets should be supervised and kept under control while around the fire. Kids and pets are naturally curious about fire and should never be left unattended when there's a fire burning. Unattended children have been known to throw all sorts of items in campfires, from aerosol cans that explode when heated to aluminum cans, which break down into dangerous aluminum dust in a campfire. We once went camping with a family who had a young child throw her Gameboy into the fire. Luckily they noticed what she'd done before she reached in to grab it.

In addition to keeping an eye on your kids and pets, it's your responsibility to keep an eye on your fire as well. A burning or smoldering fire should never be left unattended. When you're done for the night and ready to go to bed, put your campfire out. If it's hot to the touch, it's still dangerous and shouldn't be left unattended.

The easiest way to put out a campfire is with water, and it's going to take lots of it. Pour water on the campfire until it stops hissing and steaming and then stir the wet ashes and embers until you're sure everything is out.

Dirt can be added to the fire to put it out if you're trying to conserve water. Add a few shovelfuls of dirt and stir it in. Then add more and stir again. Burying a fire won't put it out. You have to continuously add dirt and stir until the fire is extinguished.

Campfire Fun

Looking for some fun and safe ways to entertain the family around the campfire? Here are some of the ways people have fun while sitting around a fire:

- **Campfire songs.** You can sing popular songs like *Kumbayah* and *Michael Finnigan* or you can bring a radio and listen to and sing family favorites.
- **Chubby bunny.** The goal of this game is to be the person who can place the most jumbo marshmallows in their mouth at once and still be able to say "Chubby Bunny." Yes, it's immature and childish. It's also fun and sure to get the whole family laughing.
- **Roast marshmallows.** Get a stick or a metal fork designed for roasting marshmallows and impale a marshmallow on the end of it. Put it close to the fire and toast it until it's golden brown. Children must be supervised while roasting marshmallows because they can catch on fire and hot marshmallow can drip and burn kids that aren't careful.
- **Roasted strawberries.** Here's one most people have never heard of. Dip a strawberry in marshmallow fluff and roast it over the campfire. These are delicious and are a good way to ensure your kids eat their fruit while camping.
- **Orange rind chocolate cakes.** Cut the top ¼ off of a large orange and scoop out the meat. You'll be left with a hollow rounded shell. Whip up a box or two of cupcake mix. Fill the orange rind ¾ of the way with batter. Place the top back on the orange, wrap

it in foil and place it in the fire. Let it cook for 15 to 20 minutes, or until the batter is cooked all the way through. Let cool for 5 minutes and serve topped with frosting or whipped cream.

- **Make s'mores.** This is a favorite of families across North America. You're going to need graham crackers, large marshmallows and milk chocolate bars. Break the graham cracker in half and place a piece of chocolate on one half. Roast a marshmallow and sandwich it between the graham cracker halves. Let it sit for 30 seconds to a minute so the chocolate will start to melt and enjoy.

- **Tell ghost stories.** Older kids will love this one. With little kids your mileage may vary. My son loves ghost stories, but a 6-year old friend of his we brought along one time hated them.

Camping Recipes

This section contains recipes you can whip up while camping. I've tried to keep them as easy as possible because most people don't want to whip up a gourmet meal while standing in a campsite. These recipes are mainly comfort foods that are filling and will replenish calories lost during a busy day, so you won't be exhausted while out and about.

Bacon, Egg, Sausage and Potato Omelet

Ingredients:
2 cups bacon, cooked and crumbled
2 cups sausage, cooked and crumbled
3 medium potatoes
½ onion
7 eggs
Salt
Pepper

Directions:

1. Fry the bacon and cook the sausage and crumble each up into chunks.
2. Slice the potatoes. Leave the peels on.
3. Dice the onion and add it to the bacon and sausage.
4. Add the potatoes to the bacon and sausage.
5. Partially scramble the eggs in a separate skillet.
6. Add the meat and the potatoes to the eggs and finish cooking.

Balsamic Barbecued Steak

Ingredients:
2 pounds Sirloin steak
1 cup balsamic vinegar
¼ cup olive oil
4 tablespoons honey
2 tablespoons garlic powder
Salt and pepper, to taste

Directions:

1. Add all ingredients except steak to a bowl and whisk together.
2. Place steak and sauce in a resealable plastic bag and shake until the steak is coated.
3. Let steak marinate for at least 6 hours.
4. Barbecue on barbecue grill or on grill placed over campfire.

BBQ Beef Ribs

Ingredients:

Ribs

Beef Glaze Ingredients:

1 cup honey

½ cup apple juice

¼ cup brown sugar

4 tablespoons Dijon mustard

Beef Rub Ingredients:

1 teaspoon salt

1 teaspoon cayenne pepper

1 teaspoon black pepper

Directions:

1. Lightly coat ribs with vegetable oil.
2. Combine salt and peppers and rub into the ribs before cooking.
3. Prepare barbecue and move hot coals to one side of the barbecue. You're going to use indirect heat to barbecue the ribs.
4. Sear the ribs by cooking them over direct heat for 2 minutes on each side.
5. Place a drip pan under the ribs and place them on the opposite side of the grill as the coals.
6. Cook ribs for 2 hours. Add new coals to the barbecue as needed.
7. Flip the ribs over and cook for another 1 to 2 hours, or until meat is ready to fall off the bone.

P a g e |**160**

8. Combine glaze ingredients.
9. Brush glaze onto ribs. Use generous amounts of glaze.
10. Cook for another 15 minutes.
11. Serve hot.

BBQ Chicken

Ingredients:
Chicken legs and thighs

Rub Ingredients:
¼ cup sea salt

¼ cup granulated sugar

3 tablespoons ground cumin

3 tablespoons paprika

1 tablespoon mustard powder

1 tablespoon chili powder

1 tablespoon cayenne pepper

1 tablespoon garlic powder

Sauce Ingredients:
¼ cup water

½ cup Worcestershire sauce

¼ cup brown sugar

1 tablespoon honey

1 tablespoon agave nectar

2 tablespoons yellow mustard

1 teaspoon soy sauce

1 tablespoon liquid smoke

Directions:

1. Add the rub ingredients to a large freezer bag and shake up until blended.
2. Place chicken in the freezer bag and shake until coated with rub.

3. Return the chicken to the ice chest and let it sit on ice for at least 3 hours. Alternatively, you can prepare the chicken and rub before you leave on your trip and put it on ice until you're ready to cook it.

4. Add all of the sauce ingredients to a saucepan and let simmer for 15 to 20 minutes, or until sauce starts to thicken.

5. Prepare barbecue by starting coals and moving them all to one side of the grill.

6. Remove chicken from bag and place on the opposite side of the grill.

7. Cook over indirect heat for 25 to 35 minutes, or until chicken starts to brown on both sides.

8. Slather BBQ sauce over the chicken pieces and place the pieces directly over the coals.

9. Cook until chicken is cooked all the way through and skin is nice and crispy. Be sure to flip the chicken regularly.

Beans and Franks

Ingredients:

6 to 10 hot dogs

5 slices bacon

2 cans kidney beans

Sauce Ingredients:

2 cans tomato sauce

½ cup ketchup

½ cup flour

1 tablespoon brown sugar

2 tablespoons Worcestershire sauce

1 teaspoon salt

Directions:

1. Cook bacon in skillet and break into pieces.
2. Add all of the sauce ingredients to a pot and stir together over medium heat.
3. Bring to a simmer and stir until the sauce starts to thicken.
4. Add the bacon and kidney beans.
5. Cut the hot dogs into coins and add them to the pot.
6. Cook until hot dogs are warmed all the way through.

Breakfast Burritos

Ingredients:
10 sausages
5 eggs
2 potatoes, peeled and cubed
1 cup cheddar cheese, shredded
Salsa
Tortillas
Non-stick cooking spray

Directions:

1. Cook sausage in a skillet.
2. Remove sausage from skillet and crumble it up or break it into chunks.
3. Slice the potatoes.
4. Spray non-stick cooking spray in skillet and brown potatoes.
5. Add sausage back into skillet, along with the eggs.
6. Cook until eggs are done.
7. Warm tortillas and fill up with the sausage, eggs and potatoes.
8. Sprinkle cheese on top.
9. Add salsa, to taste.
10. Serve warm.

Campfire Baked Potato

Ingredients:
Potatoes
Aluminum foil
Desired toppings

Directions:

1. Wash potatoes and poke holes in them with a fork.
2. Wrap each potato individually in aluminum foil.
3. Double-wrap each potato with another layer of aluminum foil.
4. Place potatoes directly on the hot coals in the campfire.
5. Bake for 30 to 45 minutes, or until potatoes are soft.
6. Let cool for 10 minutes.
7. Remove potatoes from foil.
8. Season with desired toppings and serve warm.

Clam Chowder

NOTE: This recipe can be cooked in a pot over a camp stove burner or on a heavy grill placed over the campfire. It can also be prepared in a Dutch oven, which is my favorite way to cook it.

Ingredients:

2 cans of chopped clams
2 cups half-n-half
1 cup of clam juice
1 cup water
5 thick cut slices of bacon
2 sticks of celery, chopped
1 large onion, chopped
4 potatoes, peeled and cubed
2 garlic cloves, minced

½ cup flour
1 chicken bouillon cube
½ teaspoon sea salt
½ teaspoon black pepper
½ teaspoon cayenne pepper (optional)

Bread bowls, optional

Directions:

1. Add bacon and a teaspoon of oil to the pot or Dutch oven and cook until crispy.
2. Break bacon into pieces.

3. Add onions, garlic and celery to pot and cook in bacon drippings.
4. Combine flour, water and half-n-half in a bowl and stir until smooth.
5. Add all ingredients except clams to pot or Dutch oven and bring to a rolling boil for 20 to 30 minutes, or until potatoes are soft.
6. Add clams a couple minutes before the chowder is complete. Add them too soon and the clams will get tough.
7. Serve hot. This clam chowder is absolutely delicious when served in a sourdough bread bowl.

Dutch Oven Baked Beans

NOTE: This recipe requires that you prepare the beans at home and simply reheat them when you get to the campsite. Alternatively, you can add all of the ingredients to a Dutch oven and cook them by placing the Dutch oven in the campfire, covering it with coals and letting it cook for 4 to 6 hours, or until the beans are soft.

Ingredients:

2 cups bacon, cooked and crumbled

4 cups white beans

2 onions, chopped

15 cups water

2 cups brown sugar, packed

½ cup BBQ sauce

½ cup molasses

3 teaspoons mustard

1 teaspoon garlic powder

2 teaspoons salt

1 teaspoon pepper

Directions:

1. Bring water to a boil in a large saucepan.
2. Boil beans for a few minutes until they start to soften up.
3. Add all ingredients to a Dutch oven and stir.
4. Preheat oven to 350 degrees F.
5. Place Dutch oven on bottom rack in oven and bake for 6 hours, stirring occasionally. Add water halfway through if the beans thicken up too much.

6. Store beans in a freezer bag and reheat when you want to eat them at the campsite. They go well with barbecued foods. Alternatively, you can cut hot dogs up or add smokies to them for delicious beanie weenies your kids will love.

Dutch Oven Cinnamon Caramel Monkey Bread

Ingredients:

3 canisters of Pillsbury biscuits

4 teaspoons cinnamon

1 cup brown sugar, packed

1 cup granulated sugar

1 stick butter

½ cup caramel

Directions:

1. Mix cinnamon, sugar and brown sugar together.
2. Tear biscuits into chunks and roll around in the cinnamon sugar mixture. Make sure each piece is well-coated.
3. Place the biscuit pieces in a Dutch oven.
4. Melt the butter and pour it over the top of the biscuit pieces.
5. Place lid on Dutch oven and place it in the coals of the campfire. Place hot coals on top of Dutch oven.
6. Cook for 35 to 45 minutes, or until monkey bread is cooked all the way through.
7. Remove Dutch oven from fire and let cool for 15 minutes.
8. Remove lid and drizzle caramel over the monkey bread.
9. Serve warm.

Dutch Oven Chili Macaroni

Ingredients:
2 pounds hamburger
3 cups macaroni
2 onions, chopped
3 cups diced tomatoes
1 cup tomato sauce
½ cup chilies, diced
1 teaspoon cayenne pepper
1 tablespoon chili powder
1 tablespoon dried minced onion
2 teaspoons salt

1 cup Mexican blend cheese, for topping

Directions:

1. Place Dutch oven over hot coals in campfire.
2. Let the Dutch oven heat up for 10 minutes.
3. Add hamburger and onion to Dutch oven and cook until hamburger is browned and the onions start to soften.
4. Add the rest of the ingredients and stir together.
5. Place lid on Dutch oven and cover with hot coals.
6. Let cook for 30 to 60 minutes, or until macaroni is soft.
7. Remove Dutch oven from fire.
8. Sprinkle cheese on chili macaroni as it is served.

Dutch Oven Fruit Pie

NOTE: This recipe calls for berry pie filling, but you can use cans of whatever filling you'd like. You can also make your own filling by cutting fruit and combining it with sugar and a bit of water and cooking it until it gets soft.

Ingredients:
1 can berry pie filling
1 box muffin mix
2 tablespoons butter

1 aluminum pie tin

Whipped cream, for topping

Directions:

1. Open berry pie filling can and pour contents into the pie tin.
2. Pour box of muffin mix over the top of the filling.
3. Distribute small pieces of butter over the top of the muffin mix.
4. Place the Dutch oven in the coals.
5. Set the pie tin in the Dutch oven. In order to ensure the pie cooks evenly, place a few stones in the bottom of the Dutch oven and set the pie tin on top of the stones.
6. Put the lid on the Dutch oven and cover the Dutch oven with hot coals.
7. Let cook for 15 to 20 minutes.

8. Remove pie from Dutch oven and let cool for 5 to 10 minutes.
9. Spoon fruit pie onto a plate and add whipped cream on top.
10. Serve warm.

Eggs in a Nest

Ingredients:
Eggs
Butter
Bread
Salt
Pepper

Directions:

1. Cut a hole out from the center of a slice of bread. You can use the rim of a small glass to make a clean cut.
2. Heat a skillet over medium heat.
3. Add a generous amount of butter to the skillet and let it melt.
4. Place the bread in the skillet.
5. Crack an egg and dump the contents into the hole you created in step 1.
6. Salt and pepper the egg, to taste.
7. Let the egg cook for 2 minutes and then flip the slice of bread over, keeping the egg in the hole.
8. Add a bit more salt and pepper, if so desired.
9. Let the egg cook until it reaches the desired consistency. You can cook it so the egg yolk is runny or you can leave it in long enough so the yolk gets hard.

Fire-Roasted Cinnamon Apple

Ingredients:
1 apple
½ cup sugar
1 tablespoon cinnamon
1 skewer

Directions:

1. Mix sugar and cinnamon together in a mixing bowl.
2. Push skewer into the apple.
3. Roast the apple over the open flame of a campfire.
4. Carefully peel the apple. It will be extremely hot when it first comes out of the fire, so be careful. Young children should be helped by adults.
5. Roll the apple around in the cinnamon-sugar mixture.
6. Let the apple cool a bit and eat it warm.

Five Alarm Dutch Oven Chili

WARNING: This chili has quite a kick to it and isn't for the faint of heart. It can also cause a bit of gastric distress, which is the reason why my husband has been banned from making it while we're camping. It is good, though, if spicy chili is your thing.

Ingredients:
2 pounds ground beef
3 cans pinto beans
3 cups canned diced tomatoes, with chilies
¼ cup water
½ cup tomato paste
1 large onion, diced
2 cloves garlic, minced
3 habanero peppers, seeded and diced
3 jalapeno peppers, seeded and diced

1 table spoon olive oil
3 tablespoons chili powder
2 teaspoons ground cumin
2 teaspoons oregano
2 teaspoons cayenne pepper

Directions:

1. Place Dutch oven on hot coals in the campfire.
2. Let it heat up until hot enough to brown ground beef.
3. Add 1 tablespoon of olive oil to the bottom of the oven and spread it around.

4. Add the ground beef to the oven and cook until it starts to brown.
5. Add onions and garlic and cook until onions start to turn clear.
6. Add the rest of the ingredients, except for the beans.
7. Place lid on Dutch oven and let cook for 45 minutes.
8. Remove lid and add pinto beans. Stir them in.
9. Let cook for an additional hour with the lid off.
10. Serve chili hot.

Killer Kabobs

Ingredients:
1 pound beef, cubed
1 pound chicken, cubed
1 pound shrimp, peeled and deveined
4 large bell peppers, cut into squares
4 large onions, cut into pieces
1 pound small mushrooms

Sauce Ingredients:
6 tablespoons soy sauce
6 tablespoons extra virgin olive oil
1 tablespoon garlic powder
1 teaspoon lime juice

Directions:

1. This recipe works best when the kabob ingredients are allowed to marinate in the sauce.
2. Combine sauce ingredients in a large bag and shake until blended.
3. Cut meat and veggies and place them in separate bags with the sauce.
4. Let marinate for at least 6 hours. I like to make my kabobs at home before I leave and leave them marinating in the cooler for at least a day.
5. Remove contents from bag and place them on skewers, alternating meat and vegetables. Continue until all of the meat and veggies have been placed on skewers.

6. This recipe will make 8 to 12 kabobs, depending on how much you fill them.

Quick and Easy Pancakes

NOTE: These pancakes can be cooked on a skillet or a flat metal surface placed over a barbecue grill. They can also be cooked on the inside of a Dutch oven lid. Flip the lid over and place the top of the lid in the coals. Cook the pancakes on the flat undersurface of the lid.

Ingredients:

1 cup flour
1 egg
1 cup milk
1 tablespoon melted butter
1 ½ teaspoons baking powder
¼ teaspoon salt

Vegetable oil, for cooking surface

Directions:

1. Combine all ingredients except flour and melted butter in a bowl and whisk together.
2. Add the flour slowly and stir until smooth.
3. Melt butter and stir it in.
4. Heat up cooking surface and add a small amount of vegetable oil.
5. Pour ½ cup of batter on the cooking surface.
6. Cook until the top starts to bubble and the edges start to brown.
7. Flip pancake and cook until the other side is brown.

8. Serve with your favorite toppings. Maple syrup and whipped cream are both tasty, as are many jams and jellies.

Traditional Banana Boat

Ingredients:
1 banana
5 to 10 marshmallows
1 bar of milk chocolate

Directions:

1. Peel banana.
2. Cut it in half lengthwise.
3. Place the bottom half of the banana boat on a piece of aluminum foil.
4. Use a spoon to dig a groove into the banana slice on the bottom, so it'll hold the chocolate and marshmallows.
5. Break chocolate bar into chunks.
6. Sprinkle marshmallows and chocolate chunks on the bottom half of the banana.
7. Place the top half of the banana over the bottom half and wrap in foil so the chocolate and marshmallows are held in place.
8. Place on hot coals in campfire for 10 to 15 minutes, or until the chocolate and marshmallows are melted.
9. Let cool for 5 minutes.
10. Unwrap and eat while warm and gooey.

Let's Hear Your Camping Stories

Got anecdotes or camping stories you want to share in future editions of this book? Send them to the following e-mail address:

mike_rashelle@yahoo.com

I'd love to hear from my readers. Hope you enjoyed the book! Thanks for purchasing it.

Printed in Great Britain
by Amazon.co.uk, Ltd.,
Marston Gate.